A CROCE READER

Aesthetics, Philosophy, History, and Literary Criticism

Benedetto Croce

Edited and Translated by Massimo Verdicchio

Benedetto Croce (1866–1952) was a historian, humanist, political figure, and the foremost Italian philosopher of the early twentieth century. This volume brings together new English translations and analysis of selections and excerpts from Croce's most important works in aesthetics, philosophy, history, literary criticism, and the Baroque, taking into consideration aspects of his work that have been overlooked or dismissed by scholars and critics, including Croce himself. In his introductory essay, Massimo Verdicchio traces the development of Croce as a thinker, with a focus on his philosophy of "absolute historicism" and its implications for art and culture. Unlike other anthologies of Croce's work, *A Croce Reader* includes essays from the *Aesthetics* of 1902 and key studies on Vico, Hegel, and Pirandello. Verdicchio's authoritative introduction and thoughtful selection and translation of the source material offer a fresh approach to Croce and reintroduce him as a powerful and relevant voice in literary criticism and theory today.

MASSIMO VERDICCHIO is a professor of Italian and Comparative Literature in the Department of Modern Languages and Cultural Studies at the University of Alberta.

T0341656

A CROCE READER

Aesthetics, Philosophy, History,
and Literary Criticism

BENEDETTO CROCE

Edited and translated by Massimo Verdicchio

UNIVERSITY OF TORONTO PRESS
Toronto Buffalo London

The translation and other material © University of Toronto Press 2017
Toronto Buffalo London
www.utppublishing.com

ISBN 978-1-4426-4259-1 (cloth)
ISBN 978-1-4426-1142-9 (paper)

Library and Archives Canada Cataloguing in Publication

Croce, Benedetto, 1866–1952
[Essays. Selections. English]
A Croce reader : aesthetics, philosophy, history, and
literary criticism / Benedetto Croce ; edited and translated by
Massimo Verdicchio.

Translated from the Italian.
Includes bibliographical references.
ISBN 978-1-4426-4259-1 (cloth). – ISBN 978-1-4426-1142-9 (paper)

1. Croce, Benedetto, 1866–1952.   2. Essays   I. Title.

B3614.C72E57 2017   195   C2017-901604-0

University of Toronto Press acknowledges the financial assistance to its
publishing program of the Canada Council for the Arts and the Ontario
Arts Council, an agency of the Government of Ontario.

Canada Council
for the Arts

Conseil des Arts
du Canada

ONTARIO ARTS COUNCIL
CONSEIL DES ARTS DE L'ONTARIO

an Ontario government agency
un organisme du gouvernement de l'Ontario

Funded by the   Financé par le
Government   gouvernement
of Canada   du Canada

Contents

Preface   vii

Introduction   ix

Aesthetics   3

Philosophy   19

History   39

Literary Criticism   59

The Baroque   77

Bibliography   91

Preface

This reader is unlike other readers. The aim is not to provide a selection of essays that represent the work of Benedetto Croce. Such a work already exists as an anthology in two volumes compiled by Croce himself in 1951: *Filosofia, Poesia, Storia: Pagine tratte da tutte le opere a cura dell'autore* (FPS), subsequently translated by Cecil Sprigge in 1966 as *Philosophy, Poetry, History: An Anthology of Essays*. While the *Anthology* provides lengthy essays from most of Croce's works, as the Italian subtitle indicates, *A Croce Reader* provides only selections or excerpts from some of these works. There are selections from the four major categories – "Aesthetics," "Philosophy," "History," and "Literary Criticism" – with emphasis on those passages that are significant to the understanding of other aspects of Croce's philosophy that I deal with here. These problematic passages raise issues that Croce tried to come to terms with and overcome in his lifetime, issues that are not pursued in traditional accounts.

A possible objection to *A Croce Reader* may well be that it is not a collection of essays representative of Croce's philosophy; rather it is a reader that is *critical* of his philosophy. Its aim is to bring to light the obstacles and difficulties that Croce had to confront and overcome throughout his journey as a philosopher. It does not assume, as Croce also did not, that these obstacles were ever overcome. On the contrary, by following Croce's example, it aims to shed light on the nature of these errors and on the irony inherent in every discourse of philosophy and poetry. It shows, as Croce infers, how and why a new philosophy is only a way of rethinking the old philosophy on its own terms, and how and why the error of the old philosophy becomes the truth of the new.

In the spirit of Croce's philosophy, the selections in this Croce reader represent what is "dead" in his philosophy and, for this reason, also what is "living." Hegel and Vico tell similar stories, if one is prepared to read them as such. The lessons that Croce has left to us, for the future of philosophy, aesthetics, history, and literary criticism, namely, the "residue" of his philosophy, still remain to be read.

I have not included in these selections Croce's *Philosophy of the Practical*, his political writings, and his writings on Fascism. The *Philosophy of the Practical*, whose first degree is the economic or the practical, and whose second degree is the moral activity, follows the model of aesthetics and philosophy, intuition and concept: "Economy is like the Aesthetics of practical life; morality is like the Logic" (*Estetica*, 61). Therefore, what can be said of the aesthetics can also be said of the practical. As for Croce's writings on Fascism, I have included in the bibliography two important studies by Fabio Rizi and David Roberts. I refer to the selected bibliography herein for a more detailed biography and a general introduction to his work.

I am responsible for all the translations in this volume. I have made use of existing translations in the quotations from Ariosto's *Orlando furioso*, but I have made some modifications to bring them closer to my intended meaning. I would like to thank the Croce family for kindly giving me permission to publish these selections. I also would like to thank Ernesto Paolozzi, a friend and a Croce scholar who initially assisted me in this enterprise. I would also like to thank the University of Alberta for partly supporting this project, and the University of Toronto Press for publishing *A Croce Reader*, as well as the editors, in particular Angela Wingfield, for seeing the work into print. *A Croce Reader* is dedicated to the memory of Ron Schoeffel who was a great supporter and an editor at the University of Toronto Press when this project began. Needless to say, all errors are mine.

Massimo Verdicchio

Introduction

The reason for the apparent duplication of the *Anthology* and this Croce reader is the dual nature of Croce's philosophy. Croce was not an academic; nor did he wish to be one. He was a self-made intellectual and philosopher, and he had little sympathy for academics and the way in which philosophy and literature were taught in schools. He disliked the easy formulas of university manuals that generalized and summarized these subjects without being critical. This bias, which is a leitmotif throughout his work, was formulated by Croce in an epigraph that was never used: "He took philosophy and literature from the hands of university professors" (Tolse la filosofia e la letteratura dalle mani dei professori universitari, Parente 1975). For Croce, philosophy and literature were subjects too important to be treated superficially in school manuals or left in the hands of university professors, just as valuable objects should not be left in the hands of children. Croce's radical attitude towards philosophy and literature was based on a concept of philosophy that did not exist in a vacuum and was not the expression of a single philosopher. As he saw it, the task of the philosopher was to remove the obstacles encountered by the common man in his daily pursuit of truth but which he could not resolve by his use of ordinary judgment or by his actions. In this way, the philosopher could clear the confusion and facilitate man's pursuit (of truth) and the ongoing process of culture and moral life. "A philosopher is he who removes one of these more or less serious obstacles, disperses some of these clouds, dispels the shadows, so that one may enjoy results from his work that may be either fast or slow but are always *certain* in the growing intensity of culture and of moral life" (*FPS*, 3, emphasis mine). The philosopher can err, to be sure, but his work is always ongoing because it is always being improved and continued by the other philosophers who come after him.

The work of a philosopher is inextricably bound to the philosophy of his predecessors because to do philosophy implies not feigning ex nihilo a different history that never happened but "posit[ing] oneself in relation or in connection to previous philosophies" (*FPS*, 4). Philosophy proceeds by distinguishing what is living from what is dead in every philosophy, by salvaging and furthering what is philosophically valid, and by leaving behind what is no longer viable. This is the task of every philosopher, one that always enables philosophy to renew itself. In writing about his own philosophy, in the essay "On my philosophical work" (Intorno al mio lavoro filosofico, *FPS*, 3–12), Croce had no choice but to write about Hegel, who was the last great philosopher before him, and to come to terms with his philosophy "otherwise it would have been impossible to continue [to do philosophy]" (altrimenti non si poteva andare innanzi; *FPS*, 6). A discussion of Croce's philosophy amounts, therefore, to a critique of Hegel that his detractors or his followers were unable to achieve. The former accused him of sophistry and quackery, and the latter treated his work as a Bible. In either case, this Hegel, "frozen and solidified" (congelato e solidificato), had lost all the effectiveness of the real Hegel (dello Hegel genuino, *FPS*, 5).

An example of his relation to Hegel's philosophy in which Croce capitalizes on what is "living" and discards what is "dead" is the principle of contradiction that "A is A and not not-A." This principle, according to Croce, cannot be dismissed but has to be "deeply reformed" (profondamente riformato). Since reality is not static but living and becoming, the principle of contradiction should be rather that "A is at the same time not-A." The logic of the intellect must give way to the logic of dialectics. The account of the way in which Croce became a philosopher is formulated in terms of his opposition to Hegel: how he followed Hegel's philosophy closely and where and why he departed from it. When the time came (quando suonò l'ora), he acted upon the feeling that in Hegel's philosophy there was a "hidden truth" (verità nascosta) buried under his "arbitrary system" (arbitri sistematici, *FPS*, 6), which he had to discover. This hidden truth is the "dialectic," the very logic of philosophy that Hegel had invented. This is what is "living" in Hegel, while what is "dead" is everything that "oppressed, repressed, and distorted" his thought, namely, what was not philosophical but derived from his theological and academic upbringing or from the political influences that had affected his country and his times. This Hegel is not Hegel the philosopher but the "passionate" or practical Hegel who was no longer or not yet the philosopher (*FPS*, 6). The "living" Hegel is the inventor of the dialectic; the "dead" Hegel is the builder of a closed system and the facile inventor of triads.

Hegel's great error resides in having made opposition (contrarietà) the foundation of his system, the generating principle of reality to which he reduced all forms of the Spirit by interpreting them as so many imperfect attempts at philosophical truth embodied by the "mysticism" of the Idea (*FPS*, 9). For Croce, opposites originate in the distinction that goes from one form to another, from one act of the Spirit to another, from one distinct concept to another (*FPS*, 8–9). The foundation of the unity of the Spirit is distinction, and this distinction is at one with that unity, which is but the process of distinction. Croce writes: "Poetry is poetry and not philosophy, and praxis and morality are praxis and morality and are neither poetry nor philosophy, and philosophy is philosophy and not poetry and is neither praxis nor morality; only [philosophy] nourishes itself from them and nourishes them, in turn" (*FPS*, 10).

The critique of Hegel's philosophy exemplifies Croce's philosophical work and his method of doing philosophy. The method is one of distinction and separation in which what is "living" or philosophically valid in Hegel is retained – in this case, his dialectic – and what is "dead" – its practical or empirical side – is left behind. What is living, however, is not strictly the dialectic as conceived by Hegel; this notion is itself dead because the principle of opposition that characterizes it is "abstract, static, and dead"; it is "mathematical, not organic or vital" (*FPS*, 8). Hegel's method, which binds Croce's philosophy, and which has often been criticized as neo-Hegelianism, or even as "Italian neo-Hegelianism" (*FPS*, 11) is, nonetheless, the only method to do philosophy. Only by being a "disciple" of Hegel, by following him closely, could he establish continuity with his philosophy and, where necessary, develop, correct, integrate, and substitute his theories, revise the structure of his system, and even criticize the very concept of dialectic by substituting it with his own concept of distinct forms, since these are always in motion, always dynamic and temporary. Croce's philosophy of absolute historicism aims not only at continuing Hegel's philosophy but at taking its place in the history of philosophy, if only as "a single moment in the history of thought" (*FPS*, 12). His philosophy, to be sure, will be surpassed by other philosophies, as often as he has surpassed previous ones, but the truth that he established will always remain (*FPS*, 12).

The *Anthology* exemplifies Croce's philosophy and his system of the principle of unity in distinction, which is how it has always been read. However, the essays that he collected are not without problems. In the first volume, the essay on Giambattista Vico, who had a major influence on his work, is not representative of his reading of Vico's philosophy. The essay discusses the philosophical thought *after* Vico – "The development of philosophical and historical thought after Vico" – and is not taken from *La filosofia di Giambattista Vico* (*FPS*, 16–31). Although Croce deals with Hegel in the first essay of the *Anthology*, as I have shown, the only essay on Hegel is a fictitious account of a visit paid to the philosopher in his last days by his Neapolitan disciple, Francesco Sanseverino (a Croce persona), who tells the dying Hegel what is still relevant or not in his philosophy (*FPS*, 155–74). Croce's pivotal work, the *Aesthetics* (*Estetica*) of 1902, is not even included. Instead, we find the *Aesthetica in Nuce* (*FPS*, 195–223), a general essay on aesthetics written for the fourteenth edition of the *Encyclopedia Britannica*. From *La poesia* of 1936, which is considered Croce's last major work on aesthetics, Croce does not include the key essay "L'espressione letteraria" (Literary expression), but only minor essays (*FPS*, 248–66). A surprise inclusion is the essay "Sulla natura dell'allegoria" (On the notion of allegory; *FPS*, 336–41) because allegory is not really a part of his philosophical system. On the contrary, as it will be made clear later, allegory is the bane of his philosophical system. The last section in volume 1, "History," is not apparently problematic. It includes various essays on history and excerpts from Croce's most important works – *Teoria e storia della storiografia* (*History: Its Theory and Practice*; *TSS*, 443–79), and *La storia come pensiero e come azione* (*History as the Story of Liberty*; *SPA*, 486–523) – and an important essay on the difference between Hegel's historicism and Croce's new historicism (*FPS*, 541–50).

In the second volume of the *Anthology*, besides the essays entitled "Economy" and "Ethics," there is a section on literary criticism, with chapters on Dante, Petrarch, Boccaccio, Ariosto, Goethe, and European and Italian writers. The great absent is the essay on Pirandello, but this is not surprising. As I will discuss in my section on literary criticism, Croce was not fond of Pirandello and was always very critical of his work. The second volume also includes essays that I did not include in this Croce reader: essays on political and ethical history, and excerpts from the *History of Europe in the Nineteenth Century* and from the *History of Italy from 1871 to 1915*. In the *Anthology* a section on philological criticism contains important political essays, including Croce's famous

"Anti-Fascist Manifesto of Italian intellectuals" and an essay on the Italian Liberal Party, which he founded. A miscellaneous section on philosophical and literary polemics, a section on literary and philosophical biographies, and the essay "Towards a Self-Critique" conclude the *Anthology*.

The shortcomings and discrepancies at the heart of Croce's *Anthology* make necessary a Croce reader that addresses these issues and sheds light on the other Croce that was not included in those pages and on the story of his philosophy that was never told. This Croce reader addresses a different Croce – aspects of his aesthetics, philosophy, history, and literary criticism that differ qualitatively from those of the Croce represented in the *Anthology*. This work purports to give the reader a sample of his philosophy, of its "single moment in the history of thought," and of the truth that remains.

Published in 1951, five years before the death of Croce, the *Anthology* presents his philosophy as a unified system that can still stand on its own and can be utilized as such. However, the reader of the *Anthology* is treated to the results of Croce's philosophical labours, and not to the painstaking process that led him there. Ordinarily this second aspect would be redundant because readers are more interested in the results and not in the way they are reached. In Croce's case, however, the process is more important than the results because it is here that his historico-critical method of doing philosophy – in short, his philosophy – is best illustrated. It is at this level of analysis that his critical method of distinction and separation is at work to enable his philosophy to come into being. As I have indicated, it is only in relation to another philosophy, in the relation of identity and difference that unites and separates them, that Croce's philosophy originates and unfolds.

With his *Anthology* Croce wanted to show that the process of distinction and separation, whether in the case of Hegel, Giambattista Vico, or other philosophers, though problematic, was still able to arrive at a unified system; it was simply a question of identifying the error of previous philosophies, overcoming it, and leaving it behind. This shift, however, is not unproblematic because, as Croce reminds us, the error is not a human error. The distinction between what is living and what is dead in philosophy, between poetry and non-poetry, between poetry and literature, and between symbol and allegory, is symptomatic of an impasse that is rooted in language, not in human failure. While these obstacles standing in the way of philosophy and literature appear to be resolved, they never are. These difficulties characterize the other side of the perfect embroidery of Croce's philosophical system that he gives us in the *Anthology*, and constitute the subject of *A Croce Reader* and the lesson that Croce can still teach us today. They are what remains of the truth of his philosophy and constitute what is living in its single moment of the history of thought. Although in Croce's *Anthology* the shift from past error to present truth appears to guarantee continuity and truth to philosophy, in actual fact the error is not resolved but reappears under the guise of the truth of the new philosophy. It is this truth that *A Croce Reader* denounces and exposes but also points to as the lesson that Croce can still teach us today.

A *Croce Reader* is divided in four sections: "Aesthetics," "Philosophy," "History," and "Literary Criticism." The section on aesthetics is first because the aesthetic plays a pivotal role in Croce's philosophy. As Croce reminds us in the *Aesthetics* (*Estetica*) of 1902, which is not included in his *Anthology*, knowledge has two forms: intuitive knowledge and logical knowledge; intuition and concept; aesthetics and logic. Their relation is one of degrees: expression can stand alone, but the concept cannot stand without the expression; aesthetics can stand by itself, but logic or philosophy cannot stand without the aesthetic; there is poetry without prose, but not prose without poetry (*Estetica*, 30). Croce's philosophy of absolute historicism stands and falls on this concept of aesthetics because the concept of history, which is identical to that of philosophy, depends on it as well. To these four sections I have added a fifth, on the Baroque, which is essentially a reading of Croce's *Storia dell età barocca in Italia* (History of the Baroque age in Italy), an important study that was also not selected for the *Anthology*. The work plays a seminal role in Croce's system because it is not only a history of a non-history, which is how Croce defined the Baroque age, but also a history of the age of non-poetry, or where poetry is silent. The Baroque age, in fact, can be considered the age of allegory, which for Croce was the non-poetic and a philosophical error. The *Storia dell età barocca in Italia* is also, indirectly, the history of another non-history and another non-poetry that Croce refused to write: the history of Fascism and of Futurism.

Aesthetics

Although the *Aesthetics* of 1902 brought him fame and international acclaim, Croce was never satisfied with the work owing to his inability to clearly define the concept of aesthetics, which straddles symbol and allegory. The selection from the *Aesthetics* included in *A Croce Reader* makes this clear. For Croce, following Hegel, the aesthetic is the symbol, and allegory is the error of taking the symbol as a concept. The distinction between them, however, is not easily made, because the concept of symbol is not easily differentiated from allegory.

To demonstrate that art is not imitation, Croce gives the example of wax statues. When they imitate human beings faithfully, they are not artistic. However, if an artist paints these same figures in a painting of a wax museum, we have again artistic intuition, and the composition is artistic. Framed within a painting, the wax statues can no longer be taken for human beings, and no confusion arises between art and reality. Croce's example, despite his definition of art as symbol, identifies art as allegory, which in his system is the non-artistic and an intellectual error: "We observe, likewise, that the essence of art has been thought to be the symbol. But if the symbol is conceived as inseparable from artistic intuition, it is synonymous with intuition, which has always an ideal character. Art does not have a double level [fondo], but only one level, and everything in it is symbolic because everything is ideal. But if the symbol is conceived separately, if on the one hand one expresses the symbol and on the other what is symbolized, one falls once more in the intellectual error: what passes for symbol is actually the exposition of an abstract concept; it is allegory" (*Estetica*, 39–40).

With the example of the wax statues Croce wants to show that the aesthetic is the symbol, but the example he uses proves the opposite. The artistic turns out to be what emerges not from the identity of symbol and intuition but from the discrepancy between intuition and representation, from the difference between the wax figures and the frame that contains them. This discrepancy at the core of the *Aesthetics* is never resolved, even though Croce tries to separate the symbol from allegory, or the aesthetic from other pseudo-aesthetic forms and intellectual errors. The flaw at the heart of the *Estetica* informs the *Logic* of 1909, which depends on it and turns it into a flawed logic: "A flawed Aesthetics had to lead to a flawed Logic" (Un'Estetica inesatta doveva tirarsi indietro una Logica inesatta; *Estetica*, 47). For this reason the first *Aesthetics* remains inconclusive, and probably also for this reason Croce did not include it in the *Anthology*.

The ambiguity between symbol and allegory characterizes all future discussion and attempts at defining the aesthetic until *La poesia* (Poetry, 1936). In this work Croce claims to have finally separated symbol from allegory by relocating allegory under the category of literature or rhetoric. From the selection in *A Croce Reader*, "Literary expression," which Croce does not include in the *Anthology*, it is clear that the separation is possible in name only because it is impossible to determine, from the examples he provides, where the poetic expression begins and the prosaic or literary expression ends: "Reciprocal limitations and the indissolubility of the two moments make it impossible to ever take the literary form separately and enjoy it as poetry because that form, in every word, in every position, in every rhythm, in every inflection, reveals the presence of its realistic motive, and the convenience lies in this relation" (*Poesia*, 47–8). Croce compares this condition to Goethe's bird that, after its escape from bondage, flies around the countryside with a broken thread tied to its leg, a sign that it belonged to someone (*Poesia*, 48). The broken thread is symbolic of poetry's bondage to the prosaic or to allegory, and a sign that the distinction and separation announced in *La poesia* can never take place. "Pure" poetry will always carry with it the sign of its realistic, prosaic, or allegorical origins, of its "fondo," regardless of any attempt to free it from its bondage. As for allegory, its place resides only apparently under the category of literary expression. Croce relegates it to the margins, to the notes, where he defines it as "a sort of writing or cryptography": "Amongst the forms of expression that I have reviewed I have not listed allegory, which is not a direct mode of spiritual manifestation but a kind of writing or cryptography" (*Poesia*, 227).

It is very surprising, therefore, to find in Croce's *Anthology* the essay on allegory, which is also quoted in *A Croce Reader*. As the essay makes clear, not only is allegory prosaic and non-poetic, but also it has no place in a philosophical system, except as error. Allegory is a threat to the purity of the poetic, to the philosophical concept, and to history – which for Croce is identical to philosophy – and to his philosophy of absolute historicism. If intuition cannot be distinguished from the concept, if a work of philosophy or history cannot be distinguished from a work of poetry, the very foundation of philosophy or history is in question. In these cases, rather than philosophy or history, we have metaphysics or myth, and we would have to speak of an allegory of philosophy and an allegory of history rather than a philosophy and a history.

Philosophy

The first selection of the philosophy section deals with the issue of the identity of history and philosophy. The essay marks a radical departure from Croce's earlier view of history in an essay of 1893, "History reduced under the general concept of art" (La storia ridotta sotto il concetto generale dell' arte), in which history was placed under the category of art. In the *Aesthetics* of 1902, history is said to originate at the intersection of art and philosophy, and we find a similar view in *Lineamenti di Logica* (Outline of Logic) of 1905. Later, in the *Logic* of 1909, history is said to be identical to philosophy. The passage of history from art to philosophy is, for Croce, simply the result of not having understood, at first, the real nature of history and philosophy. However, at the level of aesthetic representation, the shift is quite radical because history moves from being a symbolic form under the category of art, to a hybrid form of symbol and concept in the *Aesthetics* and in the *Outline of Logic*, to a concept in the *Logic*. A distinction and separation has taken place to resolve the error of a historical form that was neither art nor philosophy, neither symbol nor concept. The shift is similar to the one that fails to take place in the *Aesthetics*, which makes it questionable whether the distinction can now take place and history can leave its artistic or allegorical origins behind. Unless this is shown to be possible, we are only dealing with an allegory of history and an allegory of philosophy.

The other two selections illustrate Croce's historico-philosophical method of doing philosophy as applied to the philosophies of Hegel and Giambattista Vico, the two philosophers who have had the greatest impact on his philosophy. The famous essay "What Is Living and What Is Dead in Hegel's Philosophy," which I have selected for *A Croce Reader*, does not appear in Croce's *Anthology*. As I have indicated, Croce discusses Hegel indirectly in the first essay of the *Anthology* when he describes his own philosophical work. For a critique of Hegel, Croce includes the fictionalized account of a visit to the philosopher in the last days of his life by a young promising Neapolitan philosopher, Francesco Sanseverino, a Croce persona, who claims to be his disciple – "An Unknown Page of the Last Months of Hegel's Life" (Una pagina sconosciuta degli ultimi mesi della vita di Hegel). The story takes shape as a dialogue between Sanseverino and Hegel, but it is basically a monologue in which the disciple tells the master why he loves his philosophy, what the truths of his system are, and also what its flaws are. While the main problem seems that Hegel has failed to apply his dialectic correctly, Hegel is not blamed for these errors. The culprit seems to be an "evil force" (una forza maligna) that interferes with his philosophy in order to disrupt his otherwise sound and valid principles: "When I pass from the great and fertile principles that you have posited, it seems to me that an *evil force* frequently intervened to divert [stornare] those principles from their logical consequences and to compel you to accept what was intrinsically extraneous and contrary to them; worse yet, to treat it with that dialectic for which they were not suited; and, even worse, to render this dialectic superficial and mechanical by turning it to this use" (*Indagini su Hegel* [*IH*], 11–12, emphasis mine).

Hegel himself was not aware of this arbitrary interference that displaced and distorted his thought. The error could be blamed on his religious beliefs or his traditional doctrines and methods, but this would not explain the error: "To do so would be to explain the unexplainable" (avrei spiegato il non spiegabile; *IH*, 12). This kind of error is not something that can be explained or resolved, because it is something that is neither actualized nor thought, or that even happens: "any error is born from following a *different impulse* from pure thought, *an impulse of a different sort*, essentially, always interested in other ways" (*IH*, 12, emphasis mine). Croce does not elaborate on the nature of this evil force that arbitrarily undermines and distorts Hegel's system. We have to wait for his analysis of Vico's philosophy, and later of Pirandello's work, to understand what is at stake.

Croce's essay on Vico's philosophy is also not mentioned in the *Anthology*. Vico's presence is ubiquitous in Croce's work, just as Hegel's is. Sanseverino even mentions Vico to Hegel as the great Neapolitan philosopher who can be considered the precursor of his philosophy and who was even freer of religious constraints than Hegel was (*IH*, 18). This does not mean that Vico is exempt from the evil forces that create havoc in Hegel's philosophy. In the essay from the *Anthology* "Vico and the later development of philosophical and historical thought" Croce compares him to Hegel not only as one of the major philosophers of historicism but also as one who shared a similar fate: "a violent union and mingling of methods" that was responsible for many of the errors of his system (*FPS*, 126–7).

The problem with Vico's *Scienza nuova* (*New Science*), which is responsible for the obscurity and the confusion that we find in his philosophy, is caused by a lack of distinction between philosophy, history, and the empirical sciences and the way in which these are confused, and freely convert, in Vico's mind, damaging each other (*La filosofia di Giambattista Vico* [*FGBV*], 39). The culprit, once again, is an "arbitrary element that is introduced in thought and, to put it simply, is responsible for its true and real errors" (nell'elemento arbitrario che s'introduce nel pensiero, o per dirla nel modo più semplice, in veri e propri errori; *FGBV*, 39–40).

This arbitrary element is identified with a metaphorical or rhetorical language over which Vico had no control and that rendered him incapable of differentiating true philosophy from empirical elements, metaphors from concepts. Metaphors or tropes, which in the *Scienza nuova* Vico calls "monsters" (mostri; *SN* #404), have a tendency to proliferate, engendering new metaphors that in turn take on the appearance of concepts. "But metaphors are dangerous as when in the *New Science* they find fertile ground for their conversion into concepts" (*FGBV*, 58).

Croce's task in reading Hegel and Vico is to counter this evil and arbitrary force by distinguishing living philosophy from error and by re-inscribing philosophy within the history of philosophy in terms of a dichotomy of past and present or, in Vico's case, as the product of a mind that is more poetic and creative than rigorous and philosophical. In Croce's history of philosophy, Vico and Hegel become our cherished ancestors whose contributions to philosophy made it possible for his more perfect philosophy to come into being. Croce narrates this history of philosophy as the progress of the mind from its mythical and poetic origins in error to its fulfilment in the greater truth of philosophy: "The human mind ..., because of the exuberant sensual nature of primitive man and his too strong senses, unable to exercise the faculty of abstracting properties from subjects and universal forms, feigned imaginary unities, fantastic genera or myths. In its subsequent progress or development it gradually resolved the fantastic genera in intelligible genera, the poetic universals in rational ones, and freed itself of myths. *The error of myth thus passes in the truth of philosophy* [L'errore del mito passa cosí nella verità della filosofia]" (*FGBV*, 69, emphasis mine). The passage reiterates the difference that separates Vico from Croce (but also Hegel from Croce with all due modifications) and announces the birth of Croce's new philosophy from the error of Vico's philosophy or from what is dead in Hegel's philosophy. It states the successful separation of the philosophical gold from the metaphorical dross, as Croce puts it, which restores philosophical intelligibility to history: "The dross cannot be ignored as it is mixed with the gold in its pure state of nature, but it must not prevent us from recognizing and purifying the gold – or, literally speaking, history must be history, without doubt, but it is not history unless it is intelligent" (*FGBV*, 44).

The progress of philosophy from error to truth is made possible by an organic model of history in which the imaginary universals are displaced by intelligible universals, myth by philosophy, and Vico's original and creative mind by Croce's more rigorous and rational one.

The error of Vico's philosophy is thus resolved in the higher truth of Croce's philosophy: "The error of myth passes thus in the truth of philosophy." However, the sentence that announces the resolution of error is ambiguous because it can also be read another way: namely, that what was once the error of myth is now the truth of philosophy. The apparently radical, epistemological shift is only nominal; it is just a name change, from Vico's or Hegel's name to Croce's name.

In his dialogue with Hegel, Sanseverino tells him that in order to understand his theories he has to restate them in his own words: "I cannot state these truths, with the words you use and in that order, with the premises, the consequences, and the references that they present. If I had to do that, it would be best for me to keep quiet ... A philosophical sentence must be received by thought, that is, a thought by another thought, and it receives it by embracing it and wrapping itself in it [avvolgendola di sé], and only by elaborating it critically can one understand it" (*IH*, 8). Croce applies this same method to Vico. When critics complained that in his critique of the *New Science* his "interpretation of Vico was completely imbued with his own philosophical thought and therefore it was not objective" (*FGBV*, ix), Croce told them to read Vico themselves if they wanted "true" objectivity. He stated: "The historical and critical exposition of a philosopher ... has a different and higher objectivity, and it is, necessarily, the dialogue between an old and a new thought, in which only the old thought is grasped and understood. And this is what my work aimed to do. What could I have understood of Vico if I had not laboured strictly on *similar problems* to his or on problems derived from his?" (*FGBV*, ix–x, italics mine). In a later essay, from *Il carattere della filosofia moderna*, this method becomes an injunction to those not expert in philosophy who may mistake a philosophical theory for a metaphysical one and believe it to be just a pile of empty and contradictory statements. "Thus the first rule to interpret a philosophical statement is to ask against whom or against what it is polemically directed, and what 'anguish' [angoscia] it has overcome or *it has tried to overcome*" (*Il carattere della filosofia moderna* [*CFM*], 27; emphasis mine).

The problem, as Croce explains, is that unless we accept that philosophy and history are identical ("outside of this serious historical interpretation"; *CFM*, 27), philosophical theories are similar to metaphysical theories and take on "the appearance of a sequence of meaningless and contradictory assertions" (aspetto di una sequela di asserzioni vacue di significato e l'una all'altra contrastanti; *CFM*, 27).

This is how philosophical statements "appear to the profane, namely, to those who do not think by rethinking them" (come infatti appaiono ai profani, ossia a chi non pensa ripensando con esse; *CFM*, 27). The non-philosopher believes these philosophical statements to be meaningless and contradictory because he or she has not reworked them with his or her own thought, as Croce did with Hegel and Vico. In rethinking the old philosophical statements, the philosopher makes them *historical* and, therefore, meaningful and true. In so doing, the philosopher overcomes, or *tries* to overcome, the "anguish" of the error of metaphorical language that makes metaphors appear as concepts and concepts as metaphors, turning philosophy into myth or metaphysics. The process of thinking and rethinking, instead, turns philosophy into history; it makes philosophy identical to history and makes possible a philosophy of absolute historicism that rescues philosophy from metaphysics or myth.

Croce's historico-critical model is based on Vico's principle of the *verum factum*, that man can obtain proof or the certainty of the ideal eternal history by retelling or rethinking it in his own words, since man is the creator of this history and his mind possesses its guise (guisa) within the modifications of his or her own mind.

> In fact, we go so far as to claim that those who reflect on this science can narrate to themselves this ideal eternal history – since this world of nations was certainly made by men ..., and its "guise" can be found within the "modifications of his own human mind [dovendosene ritruovare la guisa dentro le modificazioni della nostra medesima mente umana]." In that proof he "had to, has to, will have to" [dovette, deve, dovrà] do it himself [esso stesso sel faccia]; because when it is the case that he who does things also narrates them, history cannot be more certain [non può essere più certa la storia]. (*Scienza nuova* #349)

History's shift from art to philosophy, and its identity with philosophy, makes it possible to establish the certainty of both philosophy and history, as distinct from the degraded forms of myth and metaphysics. By rethinking Vico's and Hegel's philosophies, in terms of "similar problems" they have in common, it is possible to re-propose them and recreate them historically in Croce's new philosophy. This is how Croce attempts to resolve the anguish of the philosopher whose metaphorical language threatens to turn his philosophy into a pile of empty and contradictory statements. In fact, the "similar problems" that Croce, Vico,

and Hegel have in common are caused by the metaphorical or tropological language that causes havoc with their philosophies.

However, the solution comes at a price. Vico explains that while
the proof of the certainty of history will give readers a divine pleasure because only in God is possible the identity of the *verum factum*, of
knowledge and action, and of philosophy and history (*Scienza nuova*
#349), this is only possible metaphorically in man at the cost of non-
understanding. If reasoned metaphysics (metafisica ragionata) or philosophy teaches man that "by understanding, man makes everything"
(*homo intelligendo fit omnia*), an imagined or poetic metaphysics (metafisica fantasticata) teaches that "by not understanding, man makes everything" (*homo non intelligendo fit omnia*; Vico's italics). The latter is the
case with Vico's philosophy: "Man by understanding unfolds his mind
and understands things, but by not understanding he makes the things
out of himself [egli di sé fa esse cose], and by transforming himself
in them he becomes them [col transformandovisi, lo diventa]" (*Scienza
nuova* #405). While a reasoned metaphysics, or a philosophy, entails
the anguish of the metaphorical or tropological language that Vico
calls, as I have indicated, monsters, an imagined or poetic metaphysics provides man with a divine pleasure because it gives him the illusion that concepts are concepts and not metaphors, but at the cost of
non-understanding.

For this reason, for Vico it is important that his readers obey the dic-
tates of his *Scienza nuova* and do not stray beyond the boundaries of
reason that he has set for them with his Principles. The risks for those
who do stray are great: "And whoever wants to stray [from the boundaries of human reason] should be careful not to go beyond humanity"
(E chiunque se ne voglia trar fuori, egli veda di non trarsi fuori da tutta
l'umanità; *Scienza nuova* #360). Those who do are comparable to the
early people who were unable to abstract forms or properties from their
subjects and who created, with their logic, monsters and poetic trans-
formations by arbitrarily combining these forms or by destroying one
subject in order to separate it from its opposite that was introduced
arbitrarily: "Hence with their logic they had to compose subjects in
order to compose these forms, or destroy a subject in order to separate its earlier form from the contrary form that was introduced." These
poetic monsters (mostri poetici), the same monsters with which Croce
and Hegel have to deal, generated in Vico's text the human monsters
that Roman law compared to the offspring of prostitutes whose nature
was human but had the qualities of animals because they were born

of vagabonds or of uncertain unions. The same is true of the monsters who were the offspring of honest women, but born outside of wedlock, "whom the Law of the XII Tables ordered to be thrown into the Tiber" (*Scienza nuova* #410). The threat and violence inherent in Vico's warning does not have an equivalent in Croce's admonition except for the dire implications, as I indicated earlier, that those who are not versed in philosophy should beware of how they approach and read philosophy lest they become like the sceptic who sits on the pile of ruins of philosophy, laughing his "inane laughter" (e lo scetticismo si asside sul cumulo delle loro rovine, ridendo del suo riso insulso; *CFM*, 27).

Croce's warning, however, echoes Vico's answer to the reviewer of the *Scienza nuova* who had questioned the theoretical validity of the work, claiming that "it indulged more in ability than in truth" (ingenio magis indulget quam veritati; *Saggio sullo Hegel*, 274). In "La dottrina del riso e dell'ironia in Giambattista Vico" (The theory of Laughter and Irony in Giambattista Vico), Croce quotes from the response made by Vico in *Vici vindiciae* (*Saggio sullo Hegel*, 274–80) where he compares his detractors, whom he calls "mockers" (derisori), to animals who perversely distort philosophical truth with their mockery: "But mockers [derisori] differ greatly from grave men [philosophers], and more than anyone they are like animals because they corrupt, or worse, they pervert the very appearance of truth and, by forcing themselves, their mind, and the truth ... what in itself is one, they twist it into something else [torcono ad altro]" (*Saggio sullo Hegel*, 277). Vico is defending not just his own philosophy from the charges of sceptics, who make fun of philosophers, the grave men of science, but also philosophy in general. Ironically, Croce's highly controversial reading of the *New Science*, questioned mainly by Vico scholars, is an example of the type of reading that Vico expects from his readers: to read the *Scienza nuova* in their own words, to re-create it in their own mind, thus making their own history – and, in Croce's case, his own philosophy of absolute historicism. Croce's accusations of obscurity and confusion in Vico's philosophy are an important critical strategy to correct and resolve the rhetorical interferences of tropes (or monsters) that plague Vico's philosophy, by reformulating his thought in his more rigorous philosophy. Only in Croce's philosophy can we say that Vico's *New Science* has overcome the anguish of rhetorical or tropological language and survives as philosophy. The same can be said of Hegel's philosophy of absolute idealism that becomes truly philosophy only when it is re-thought in Croce's new philosophy of absolute historicism.

History

In the previous section I alluded to the major shift that the concept of history undergoes from art to philosophy, and the implications of the identity of philosophy and history for Croce's philosophy of absolute historicism. This problematic also informs his other writings on history. In *Teoria e storia della storiografia* (*History: Its Theory and Practice* [*TSS*]) it appears as the distinction between chronicle and history to show that all history is contemporary history. Contemporary history is contemporary not in the literal sense of the word but in the sense that history relates to life in a relation of unity, in the sense that life relates to thought, as document to narrative, as life to history. When this link is broken, we no longer have history but chronicle, that is, only empty words, empty names, empty judgments, and empty subjects. History and chronicle are two spiritual modes, one of which is alive, the other dead; one is an act of thought, the other an act of will; one is rational, the other irrational; one is philosophy, the other myth or allegory. However, what is chronicle and dead today – as are so many documents that are "silent" to us today – can come back to life and speak again. This is because "the spirit is itself history" (*TSS*, 27): it contains the entire history within itself, and in every moment it "makes history" (il fattore di storia), which is not only the result of all previous histories but also coincides with itself (coincide poi col sé stesso; *TSS*, 27). As Vico points out, history is the only science of which man can have certainty because man makes history, and therefore man can know it, and its guise can be found in man's mind. When the *factum* coincides with the *verum*, and philosophy combines with philology, they produce history.

In the second selection, from *La storia come pensiero e come azione* (*History as the Story of Liberty* [*SPA*], at issue is the distinction between transcendental philosophy and history. For Croce, together they form a unity, but whenever philosophy is taken in isolation, it is no longer philosophy but metaphysics, no longer living but dead. The philosophy of history, for which Croce criticizes Hegel, was never history but chronicle, just as his philosophy was never philosophy but metaphysics: "The 'philosophy of history' was the result of a mental impotence or, to say it with Vico, the result of a 'lack of the mind' ('inopia della mente'), similar to myth" (*SPA*, 29). Vico's philosophy, and the philology that accompanied it, failed because of a lack of passion and interest and because it was not the result of "occasion" (di occasione), as Goethe said of poetry;

whereas poetry has to be "passionate," history and philosophy must be "practically and morally motivated" (*SPA*, 30).

The third selection is taken from a collection of essays on history and philosophy, *Il carattere della filosofia moderna* (The character of modern philosophy) [CFM]. The essay selected, "Il concetto della filosofia come storicismo assoluto" (The concept of philosophy as absolute historicism), focuses on the distinction between metaphysics and philosophy that makes possible the definition of Croce's philosophy as "absolute historicism." The fine line that differentiates metaphysics from philosophy is history, as I indicated earlier. As Vico theorizes in the passage I have just quoted from *La storia come pensiero e come azione*, history is the only science of which man can have certainty, so only history can give philosophy the certainty that metaphysics does not have. This explains why Hegel's philosophy of absolute Spirit is a metaphysics and an allegory of philosophy, and Croce's philosophy is a philosophy of absolute historicism.

Literary Criticism

The selections on Dante and Ariosto are different from those chosen for the *Anthology*. For Dante, Croce selected only the last chapter from *La poesia di Dante* (*The poetry of Dante*), the "Carattere e unità della poesia di Dante" (Character and unity of Dante's poetry), which is a summary of his analysis of the three cantiche that emphasizes the unity of the poem. My selection, "On the structure and poetry of the *Commedia*," focuses instead on the polemical character of his analysis of Dante's *Commedia* that differentiates between poetry and structure, the poetic and the allegorical. The distinction and separation of the poetic from the non-poetic reiterates the distinction of symbol and allegory, with the aim of excluding allegory as the non-poetic.

The selection for Ariosto is also different. The selection in the *Anthology* comes from the chapter "Concept of Harmony" on how the concept of harmony works in *Orlando furioso*, whereas my selection is taken from "Sommo amore: L'Armonia" (Harmony: The highest love). *Armonia* is the name Croce gives to Ariosto's irony, a notion he does not approve of because of the radical implications of Romantic irony for art, and of Pirandello's brand of irony, "umorismo" (humour). Instead of irony, a rhetorical trope, whose function is to "disrupt and destroy art" (*Ariosto*, 48), Croce prefers the term *Armonia*, which remains rigorously "within the confines of art," and conceives of "destruction" in the philosophical sense of "conservation" (*Ariosto*, 55). Croce compares Harmony to the painting technique of "veiling a colour" (velare un colore), which entails toning down a colour (smorzarlo di tono) rather than erasing it (*Ariosto*, 57). In the story of Isabella, for instance, her death does not plunge the poem into tragedy but keeps it within a "general and perpetual harmonic catharsis" (*Ariosto*, 59).

The third selection focuses on the work of the dramatist Luigi Pirandello, who is not mentioned in the *Anthology*, for good reasons. Besides the repeated squabbles in their lifetime, Croce never concealed his dislike of Pirandello and his work, which he made known in his essay on the author, "Luigi Pirandello," in *La letteratura della nuova Italia* (The literature of the new Italy [*LNI*]), partly included here. The reference to humour (umorismo) is to Pirandello's brand of irony and to a famous essay by that name, "L'umorismo," which outlines a theory of humour or irony. Croce defined Pirandello's work as neither art nor philosophy because of his tendency, in the novels and in the plays, to over-intellectualize or "pseudo-philosophize," as he called it, issues of individual life experience in order to assert universal, philosophical truths, with the result that acceptable good art was "stifled or disfigured by his inconclusive philosophizing" (*LNI*, 337).

Although Pirandello was a novelist and a dramatist, his flaws are not unlike those of Hegel and Vico; they are the result of a rhetorical or metaphorical interference, comparable to Hegel's evil force and Vico's arbitrary element and responsible for similar categorical errors that disrupt the distinction between intuition and concept and between art and philosophy. This rhetorical or tropological language's "tendency to interfere" is illustrated in Croce's analysis of Pirandello's play *Trovarsi* (To find oneself), about an actress who does not know who she is and whether she is acting in real life as she is on stage, and who wants to find herself. For Croce the play works as long as it remains within its given poetic limits, as long as "it has its own sense and use." However, when it is posited as a general philosophical problem of whether the self can be found in art or in life, and no longer as a poetic problem, it is no longer acceptable. For Croce it is not even an issue, because the self can be found not just in life and on stage but in any other human activity: in politics, in economy, and even in philosophy. However, as Croce writes this, his analysis takes a sudden turn, and, instead of focusing on the self and how one can find it anywhere, he writes about the tendency of rhetorical language to interfere with discourse everywhere, and how one must always be on guard against this interference; and if one is interfered with, one must become aware that what he is doing at present is different from what he was doing before:

> But, put in terms of a general problem, if the self can be found in life or in art, what else can one reply, without fussing too much [senza tanto smaniare], but that one can find it in one as well as in the other, and not only in actresses, not only in theatre, not only in art, but in every specific activity (in politics, in economy, and even in philosophy), *there looms* [si profila] *the tendency to interfere, with the habit of a special experience, in the exercise of all remaining life; for this reason we must always be vigilant* [vigilare] *and, in case, come to our senses* [riscuotersi] *and realize that what is in front of us now, what we must do, is of a different nature from what we were doing before.* (LNI, 366–7, italics mine)

Although he tells us to be vigilant, Croce himself is not aware that he is being interfered with, and he does not know that what he is doing now is different from what he was doing before. The passage allegorizes the workings of the rhetorical or tropological language that interferes and disrupts arbitrarily not only philosophical discourse, as we have seen in the case of Hegel and Vico, but also literary and critical discourse. At issue is not whether the mind is creative or rigorous, poetic or philosophical, old or modern, as Croce claims in his analyses. Rhetorical language intrudes to undermine the discourse of philosophy or literature, independently of the mind, which, as in this case, is always unaware that it is being interfered with. It is impossible to be vigilant over this language and to know where one is and that one is doing something different from what one was doing before.

In rhetoric the name of this disruption is *anacoluthon*, a figure of irony, which disrupts and suspends the logic of discourse permanently – a "permanent parabasis," as Friedrich Schlegel defined it. In the essay on Ariosto, the term *Harmony*, chosen by Croce to describe Ariosto's irony, has a levelling function only at the level of theme and character development but not at the level of language. In Pirandello, irony, "umorismo," or humour, targets principally the self, which turns out to be a linguistic construct, a grammatical subject, which is undone by irony. In the essay on humour ("L'umorismo") Pirandello defines it as the shadow that undermines the body, or the self, by making fun of its claims of knowledge and permanence: "Humour consists in the feeling of opposites [sentimento del contrario] produced by the special activity of reflection, which does not remain hidden and does not become, as it usually does in art, a form of feeling; it becomes its opposite, though it follows closely behind the feeling, as the shadow follows the body. The ordinary artist only pays attention to the body; the humorist pays attention to both, and sometimes more to the shadow than to the body" ("L'umorismo" ["On Humour"], 160). The humorist or the ironist pays more attention to the discrepancy between the shadow and the body, that is, the qualitative difference between the claims made by the self and the substance of those claims. It is mainly in Pirandello's prose works that we find examples of the disruptive character of "umorismo," as in the novel *Il fu Mattia Pascal* (*The Late Mattia Pascal*), which Croce described as "a funny little novel" (a piccolo romanzo scherzoso) that could have had the title "Il trionfo dello stato civile" (The triumph of the welfare state; *LNI*, 359). In the novel, however, it is not the state that triumphs, but irony, which undermines at every turn the attempts of the main character, Mattia Pascal, to "change [him] self," to invent a new identity and a new life for himself. The word *fu* (was) in the title, meaning "late" or "dead" when attached to a name, can be understood as another name for *irony*, which, by continuously disrupting and undermining Mattia Pascal's plans to change his status, turns him from a living to a dead man.

The Pirandello essay both demonstrates and confirms the issues at the heart of Croce's philosophy that he attributed to shortcomings in Vico and Hegel and to flaws in their philosophies. In distancing himself from them, Croce wants to claim that their works are empty or dead narratives or allegories, while the "error," or what is dead, becomes the truth of what is living as philosophy. However, as I have shown, neither Croce nor his philosophy is immune from the disruptive effects of this language or from irony. The attempt to relegate allegory to a past that is dead and that can be left safely behind is only another beautiful lie, an allegory of the impossibility of philosophy to free itself of allegory and irony. As Goethe's bird, mentioned earlier, philosophy and poetry will always carry with them the sign of their allegorical origins, and language will always remind them of it through irony, as the humorist knows only too well. To conclude, my aim has not been to criticize Croce or to point to any failure in his philosophy; on the contrary, it has been to point to a problem of philosophy, which affects all philosophers and philosophies alike, and that Croce was instrumental in pointing out in his efforts to resolve it. This is Croce's legacy and what he can still teach us today.

The issues that we have outlined in the four categories of "Aesthetics," "Philosophy," "History," and "Literary Criticism" all have their roots in the *Estetica* of 1902, which is an even more radical work than it has been given credit for. As the full title of *Estetica* makes clear, aesthetics is equated with language: "Aesthetics as science of expression and general linguistics" (*Estetica come scienza dell'espressione e linguistica generale*). There have been a few attempts at working out an independent theory of his linguistics, but the identity of aesthetics and linguistics is made very clear in the concluding chapter of the *Aesthetics*. Croce compares the philosophers of aesthetics and linguists to labourers working on the same tunnel from opposite ends. At a certain point the linguists must hear the voices of their co-workers, the philosophers of aesthetics, who are working from the other side: "At a certain level of the scientific process, linguistics as philosophy must fuse with aesthetics. And it does fuse *without leaving a residue*" (E si fonde, infatti senza lasciare residui; *Estetica*, 166, italics mine). The identity of aesthetics and linguistics entails a conception of language as symbol, and it is exemplified by the identity of intuition and expression on which Croce's entire system depends.

The subtitle of the *Aesthetics* was written in reaction to Hegel's *Aesthetics* (*Vorlesungen über die Ästhetik*), in which the apparent definition of the aesthetic was the symbol, but its language was far from symbolic. As I have indicated, Croce thought that Hegel's philosophy was a metaphysics, and his philosophy an allegory. The identity of aesthetics and linguistics "without … a residue" was meant as a corrective to Hegel, but, as I have shown, the relation of aesthetics and linguistics always and inevitably leaves a "residue." The example of the wax figures, instead of supporting a concept of aesthetics as symbol, points to a concept of aesthetics as allegory. Whenever identity is posited, whether in philosophy, history, or literature, it is always possible to read in it a residue that undermines its claim.

This residue is the string tied to the leg of Goethe's bird, which denounces the allegorical or prosaic origins of pure poetry. Croce, after Hegel, defined allegory as a form of writing, a cryptography, that can exist on its own, while the symbol cannot exist without the allegory on which it depends and which is its ephemeral and illusory counterpart. The difference between the two, however, is elusive and undecidable.

In the *Estetica* Croce gives an example of the confusion that exists between symbol and allegory, between the artistic and the anti-artistic, when deciding what is artistic. In describing two different paintings, people will employ both terms interchangeably:

> For instance there will be someone who, in front of two paintings – one without inspiration, where the author has copied, not very cleverly, natural objects, and the other, well inspired but not comparable to existing objects – will call the first realistic and the second symbolic. Vice versa, others, in front of a painting that is strongly felt and portrays a scene of daily life, will utter the word "realistic," and, before a painting that coldly allegorizes, [will utter] the word "symbolic." It is evident that in the first case "symbolic" means artistic, and "realistic" means the anti-artistic, whereas in the other case "realistic" is synonymous with artistic, and "symbolic" with anti-artistic. Is it any wonder, then, that some claim, most heatedly, that the true artistic form is the symbolic and that the realistic is the anti-artistic, and others that the artistic is the realistic and that the anti-artistic is the symbolic? And how can we decide who is right or who is wrong when they employ words with meanings so different from one another? (*Estetica*, 78–9)

When reading Croce, we cannot take for granted what he means by the grammar of his philosophical statements. The essays in his *Anthology* cannot be read as saying what they appear to be saying. His work cannot be read symbolically but has to be read allegorically, that is, despite or against itself, as a text that does not mean what it says. The essays selected by Croce for the *Anthology* were meant to be representative of his work and to be read as exemplifying the unity of his philosophy of absolute historicism. Yet these essays also leave a residue that tells a different story, a story that undermines this happy conclusion, as long as we are willing to read the "other" story that it inevitably and necessarily reveals. A good example is Croce's selection of the essay "On the Nature of Allegory" for the *Anthology*. Of all the essays from his entire corpus this one is not only the least representative of his work but also the one that should not be included in these essays. Its inclusion, however, is once again an example of language's "tendency to interfere"; it is the residue that undermines and perverts the conception of philosophy that it claims to promote. Its presence among the other essays is one more indication of the impossibility of excluding allegory and of banishing it to the margins, as Croce attempts to do throughout his work. Allegory can be banished in name only because neither philosophy nor poetry can exist without it. To slightly alter Croce's claim, we could say that aesthetics fuses with linguistics by leaving a residue, and the name of the residue is *allegory*.

In the *Taccuini di lavoro*, his working diaries, Croce wrote that he made three major contributions to philosophy and culture, namely, he established that (1) philosophy is methodology, and nothing else, which in this case is everything; (2) every history is contemporary history; and (3) art is lyrical intuition (and, as a result, literary and artistic history are individual and personal (Sasso, *Per invigilare me stesso*, 86). So far I have discussed two of Croce's contributions but I have not touched upon the third one, the contribution to the lyrical character of art. Croce is referring specifically to an article that he wrote in 1908, "L'intuizione pura e il carattere lirico dell'arte" (Pure intuition and the lyrical character of art), which was published in *La critica* that same year and was reprinted in *Problemi di estetica* [PE] in 1954. This little-known essay was obscured by his later contributions in *La poesia* of 1936 where he also dealt with "pure poetry" (poesia pura) but did not identify it directly with the lyrical character of art. Clearly, the essay did not receive the attention that Croce expected because it is a more modest version of what he had already written in the *Estetica* of 1902.

After outlining five possible aesthetics, Croce establishes the possibility of a "return" to a Romantic aesthetic as the only viable one and superior to all other aesthetics, which "ideally" (idealmente) goes even beyond Kant's doctrine (*PE*, 10). For Croce, however, it is not simply a question of returning to a Romantic aesthetics as we know it but to what he calls a doctrine of pure intuition or pure expression (which is the same). In fact, a return to just a Romantic aesthetics would entail falling into the aporias that led to the famous paradoxes of "art-irony" and the "death of art," and to the impossibility of ever resolving the problem of the nature of art (*PE*, 12).

Whereas in *La poesia* Croce was looking for a place in which to locate the prosaic or allegory, which he found in the category of literature, he is now looking for a place in which to relocate the aesthetic of pure intuition or pure expression and finds it in a revamped Romantic aesthetics. Differently from history and philosophy, art stands solely on fancy (fantasia), and its only patrimony are images (*PE*, 14). Art does not classify objects, it does not make them real or imaginary, and it does not qualify or define them: "it feels them and represents them. Nothing more"

(li sente e rappresenta. Niente di più; *PE*, 14). Art is pure intuition and
nothing more. "And therefore, in so far as it is concrete knowledge (and
not abstract knowledge), which grasps the real without alterations and
falsifications, art is intuition; and in so far as it posits it in its immediacy,
not yet mediated and clarified by the concept, it is pure intuition" (*PE*, 14).

In being pure, naked, and poor lies the strength of art. The example
that Croce gives is borrowed from Vico. In the first instant that man
opens to theoretical life, he clears the mind of any abstraction and any
reflection, and in that purely intuitive moment he could only be a poet:
"he contemplated the world with eyes naive and full of wonder, and
he plunged deeply into that contemplation and lost himself" (*PE*, 15).
Thus, art opens the way to knowledge by continuously refreshing the
aspect of things and "perpetually turns us into poets" (*PE*, 15). Art is
at the root of all our theoretical life, and as such it makes possible the
flower and the fruit of knowledge or of philosophy (*PE*, 15).

The distinction between art and not-art is drawn, as we find it in the
Estetica, along the lines of symbol and allegory, although here Croce
does not use these terms. Croce's term for symbolic art is *life*, namely,
"the movement, the commotion, the warmth, the feeling [sentiment]
of the artist" (*PE*, 17). By contrast, allegorical art lacks the personality
at whose contact the spectator or the reader can warm himself; it is
"cold" (fredda; *PE*, 18) and generates in us the regret for what might
have been. An allegorical work, a wrong work (un'opera sbagliata), is
one that is "incoherent," in which there is not just one personality but
many that are "disruptive" (disgregato) and "in conflict" (cozzante); in
the final instance, this amounts to "effectively none" (effettivamente
nessuna; *PE*, 18).

The issue of personality is an essential element of the work of art, but
it also creates problems when there are more "personalities" at work
that disrupt and contradict one another: "It is said that the bad artist
leaves traces of his personality in the work of art, whereas the great
artist erases them all [le cancella tutte]. [It is said] that art must portray
the reality of life and not disrupt it [turbarla] with opinions and judgments and personal feelings of the author; that the artist should give
us the tears of things and not his own tears; thus the character of art
has been said to be not personality but, in fact, precisely the opposite,
impersonality [l'impersonalità]" (*PE*, 18). In the last instance, the difference between personality and impersonality matters little because the
theory of impersonality does not differ qualitatively from the theory of
personality. What is more pressing for Croce is the interference or the

disruption of the empirical personality of the artist that clashes with the spontaneous and ideal personality of the work: "The opposition of those artists, critics, and philosophers was directed against *the invasion* [invasione] *of the empirical personality* willed by the artist in the ideal and spontaneous personality that constituted the subject of the work of art" (*PE*, 19, italics mine). The invasion characterizes the work of those artists who are incapable of representing things in themselves and feel the need to add devices that better illustrate the feelings that they were unable to represent: "For instance, those artists who, unable to represent the power of pity or the love of country, add to their faded images speeches or theatrical devices, with the idea, in so doing, of arousing those feelings, that is, similar to rhetoricians and actors who introduce into the work of art a commotion foreign to the one intrinsic to the work itself" (*PE*, 19). The "invasion" that Croce regrets is precisely the "art-irony" that he wanted to avoid in adopting a Romantic aesthetics. The reference to theatrical devices is to the technique of aside or parabasis in comedy, as described by Friedrich Schlegel, namely, the interruption of the dramatic action when the author, or an actor, provides a commentary on the action of the play.

For another example of impersonal art, Croce mentions naturalist works that, in so far as they can be considered works of art, have their own personality, even though they are characterized by a "disorientation" (smarrimento) or an "uncertainty" (perplessità) of the values of life, and by a blind faith in the natural sciences or in modern sociology. However, where they lack a personality, which has been replaced by the pedantic claim to gather human documents or to describe social conditions or the development of disease, the work of art is also lacking. This type of impersonal art is equally suspect. While it gives an exact reproduction of reality, in its empirical development, and consists of ingenious and indifferent combinations of images, it is bothersome (fastidio) and it is not artistic (*PE*, 19).

For Croce both pure intuition and the personality of the artist are necessary. The work of art requires both "the classical moment of perfect representation or expression" and "the Romantic moment of feeling." Art cannot just be "naive" or "sentimental"; it has to be both. If it has to be epic or lyrical, it has to be both: "poetry and art must be epic and lyrical together or, if one prefers, dramatic." These are all elements that do not refer to separate types of art but "must be found, necessarily, united in every work of art, even though they are different under any other aspect" (*PE*, 20).

However, since the essence of art is theoretical, the fact that it is also intuition presents a difficulty because art cannot be both theoretical and practical – that is, feeling, personality, and passion. This art then would be allegorical, and this is entirely unacceptable: "affatto insostenibile" (*PE*, 21). The duality inherent in art, its intuitional and lyrical character, must be "destroyed" (distrutta) and "proven illusory," or we have to move to a wider and more comprehensive conception of art in which intuition is only a secondary or a particular aspect. For Croce, this is possible only if we can show that form is content and that pure intuition is itself "lyrical" (*PE*, 22). This, indeed, is what is true: "Very well, this is precisely the truth: pure intuition is essentially lyrical" (*PE*, 22). The problems we have encountered to this point arise because we have not fully understood this concept. When we do, we become aware that "from one breast the other arises, or, better, one and the other are revealed as one and the same" (*PE*, 22). That is why the origin of language has been identified with the "interjection" (interiezione; *PE*, 23). Aristotle suggested, instead, "invocation" or "prayer," and he added that this type of proposition is not part of logic but belongs to rhetoric and to poetics. A landscape is a mood or a feeling, and it can be expressed in an exclamation of joy, pain, admiration, or regret: "The more a work of art is objective the more it is poetically subjective" (*PE*, 23).

However, we do not readily accept this definition of art as being pure intuition and lyrical because we are unable to differentiate between fancy (fantasia) and imagination. The two are only apparently identical. Not only are they different, but they also need to be kept distinct and separate. Fancy belongs to the poet, but imagination is excluded from art because it is responsible for "new and bizarre" ways and for arbitrary combinations of images. Imagination is unreliable because it can create objects that do not exist in the world, like monsters or animals with the head of an ox and the body of a horse:

If one fashions, arbitrarily, *stans pede in uno*, any image by attaching, for instance, the head of an ox onto the body of a horse, is this an intuition, and a pure intuition completely deprived of any conceptual reflection? And is the result a work of art, or is it, at least, artistically motivated? Certainly not. But the image used as an example, and any other produced by the imagination, not only is not pure intuition but is not even a theoretical product. It is an arbitrary product ..., and an arbitrary aesthetic object is foreign to the world of contemplation and thought. We could say that the imagination is a practical device or play that is applied to the wealth of

images belonging to the spirit, whereas fancy, which translates practical
values into theoretical ones, moods into images, is the creation of this very
same property. (*PE*, 24–5)

Hence an image that is the expression of a feeling or a mood is not even
an image; it has no theoretical value, and therefore it does not constitute
an obstacle to the identity of lyric and intuition.

The other major problem confronting Croce and the identity of pure
intuition and the lyrical is metaphysics. If any perception of a physical object can be said to be aesthetic, then intuition and the lyrical are
no longer necessary components of a work of art. These perceptions,
however, are not aesthetic, because they are not pure intuitions. But
they could be considered aesthetic in the event that the pure intuition
of a physical object with which we are dealing were a metaphysical
reality: "a reality truly real, and not just a construction or an abstraction of the intellect" (*PE*, 25). Man in his first theoretical moment would
intuit, at the same time, himself and external nature, spirituality, and
the physical object (*PE*, 25). However, in this case, we have a dualism,
and on these bases we cannot have a coherent aesthetics. This dualism
is repugnant both to aesthetics and to philosophy and has to be rejected
(*PE*, 26).

Croce shows, nonetheless, that when man moves from art to thought,
or to the concept, he does not abandon its practical and volitional base;
he still finds himself in a mood whose representation, which accompanies necessarily the movement of ideas, is still intuitive and lyrical.
This persistence of the artistic element in logical thought does not form
a dualism, because a relation of degree is not a class relation: "Copper
is copper whether it is by itself or combined to make bronze" (*PE*, 27).
However, this statement is contradicted by the many analyses in which
Croce attempts to separate precisely the empirical from the philosophical. In his reading of Vico, as I have indicated, he states that philosophy
is philosophy only if it can be separated from the dross with which it is
combined. In this case, copper is copper, but when it is combined, it is
really bronze.

The truth value of this statement brings up the issue of the "sincerity" that we require of the artist, and of the philosopher, which implies
that the artist has a mood or a feeling to express, one that he himself has
experienced and not just imagined – because imagination, as we know,
does not lead to truth. Sincerity does not go beyond the expression of a
feeling or a mood. Art is indifferent to any reason that may underlie the

experience of the artist, whether it be a desire or a mood. This attitude of indifference and non-discrimination is also characteristic of art with respect to philosophy and history. Croce quotes Aristotle once again to the effect that art does not differentiate between truth and falsehood: "Art, in fact, captures the throbbing reality, but it does not know that it does, and therefore it does not really capture it; it is not bothered by abstractions of the intellect and therefore it does not fall into falsehoods, but it does not know that it does not" (*PE*, 28).

Croce's principal aim in the essay was to establish art as the first and the most naive form of knowledge and that art could not be considered the ultimate goal of the theoretical spirit. When we read the poetry of the poets and observe the paintings of the painters, we have the impression that only in art and in aesthetic contemplation there is truth, especially with respect to the abstractions of the sciences that, as such, are completely devoid of truth. Art "has the superiority of its own truth, however simple, small, and elementary it is" (*PE*, 29–30). The essay was meant, mainly, for those who attributed theoretical relevance to art forgetting that philosophy was the form of the theoretical spirit that allows us to critique science and to recognize the nature of art, and which is neither science nor art; for those who forget that philosophy is the "supreme instance of the theoretical world" (*PE*, 30). For Croce this is the "error" that continues to be made in his own day among those whom he calls the fanatics of art who believe that art is the highest form of knowledge. The underlying aim of the essay, therefore, is to re-awaken the conscience for Philosophy (la coscienza del Pensiero) in the new generation of intellectuals, the Futurists, who privileged art over philosophy, and for Croce the best way to achieve it was to define precisely the limits of art and "to construct a solid Aesthetics" (*PE*, 30).

In a note to this essay, which was first given as a talk in Heidelberg in 1908, Croce relates that the essay was a first "integration" (integrazione) of his *Aesthetics* of 1902. The second integration was the essay of 1918, "Il carattere di totalità dell'espressione artistica" (The character of totality of artistic expression), and the third integration was made with *La poesia* of 1936 where he finally differentiated between art and literature. Croce called this a process of *integration* because the principles discussed have never changed during the entire process but have only been "refined and expanded" (*PE*, 30n1). In other words, the purpose of the essay on the lyrical character of art, as well as of his other attempts to differentiate art from literature, or symbol from allegory, as we have seen, was to mark the boundaries of art by *voiding* the aesthetic of any possible element that could be construed as logical, in order to "re-awaken the conscience for Philosophy" in a generation of "fanatics of art" that downplayed the value of philosophy, and in particular Croce's philosophy – the Futurists.

In *Storia d'Italia 1871–1915* (History of Italy, 1871–1915; published in 1927), in the chapter "Rigoglio di cultura e irrequietezza spirituale, 1901–1914" (Cultural blossoming and spiritual unrest, 1901–1914), Croce takes up his complaint of the poetic generation of his time, especially of Futurism, by assessing the work being done on art and poetry. Although positivism was on the wane, the era was ruled by an excessive focus on aesthetics. Despite the publication of Croce's *Logic* in 1909, it lacked the impact of a major philosophy. This was the era of other "philosophies" like those of the decadent movement and of Gabriele D'Annunzio, which was "a conception or an interpretation of life and, therefore, in its own way, a philosophy" (*Storia d'Italia*, 314). In reviewing the art and poetry journals of the time (*Leonardo, Prose, L'Anima, and Lacerba*), Croce points to the "irrationalism" that characterized the major cultural trends in Italy and which blurred the lines between duty and pleasure, morality and utility, truth and non-truth: "In all of them [journals], besides some attempts to restrain it, oppose it, or mitigate it with ideas from different sources, the consequences proper of an irrationalism were evident, namely, the weakened or the exhausted feeling of distinction – the distinction between truth and non-truth in the theoretical sphere; between duty and pleasure, morality and utility, in practical things; between contemplation and passion, poetry and convulsion, artistic taste and voluptuous libido, in the field of aesthetics; between spontaneity and lack of discipline, originality and extravagance, in cultural life" (*Storia d'Italia*, 314). The diatribe is directed mainly at the Futurists, "the lovers of art" (gli spasimanti dell'arte), "priests of pure beauty" (sacerdoti della pura bellezza; *Storia d'Italia*, 314), who threw to the winds any logical sense and gave themselves over to the free play of the imagination. The Futurists celebrated, precisely, the opposite values to those that Croce had upheld in his essay on the lyrical character of art, imagination and allegory: "sensual figures" (sensuali figurazioni) and "frigid symbols" (frigidi simboli; *Storia d'Italia*, 314). By promoting philosophy and by defining the lyrical character of art, Croce meant to counter, precisely, the Futurists' prosaic or allegorical character of art that disrupts and suspends the claims of philosophy.

Croce's attitude towards the Futurists is similar to his prejudice against allegory. We will return to this aspect in the section on the Baroque and in the discussion of *La storia dell'età barocca in Italia*, in which a critique of the Baroque also blends with a critique of Futurism. For our present purposes, it is important to note that Croce's attitude towards the new generation of intellectuals, critics, and poets is comparable to their attitude towards Croce and his philosophy. As the major philosophical exponent of Italian culture at the time, Croce started a journal of culture and criticism called *La Critica*, which became an important voice for philosophy, literature, and culture. However, it was the publication of his *Aesthetics* in 1902 that created great commotion not only with the young generations but throughout the world: "the lessons of the *Aesthetics* ... entered in every mind, disrupting [turbando] the minds of young people and scholars, professors and academics" (*Storia d'Italia*, 319). While the *Aesthetics* and Croce became very popular, the impact on the new generation was minimal, "appreciated by a few" (non fu accolto se non da pochi; *Storia d'Italia*, 319–20). As Croce narrates in his *Storia d'Italia*, his work was misunderstood and appreciated only in part. The unity of his philosophical system was often fragmented and reduced to pieces, and these pieces were often "disfigured [stravolti] with a meaning that was not their own," as he recounts in the third person the case of his "aesthetic formulas [dottrine], which ... were distorted into modernist formulas in order to justify the most confused and decadent Romanticism or 'Futurism,' and which Croce not only condemned on the bases of his own theories but personally abhorred with his whole being" (*Storia d'Italia*, 320).

Croce attributes the reason for the lack of a positive reception of his philosophy to an "impetuous current of irrationalism that, from life, penetrated the philosophy of his time and obscured it [intorbidiva]" (*Storia d'Italia*, 320). This is an indirect allusion to the wave of irrationalism that brought about Fascism, which affected culture and the arts, to the advent of Futurism and to the philosophy of Gentile, a philosopher, long-time friend of Croce, and once his collaborator on *La Critica*: "[Croce] saw, suddenly, rising next to him a form of irrational idealism represented by one of his collaborators [Gentile] who had been instrumental in promoting the study of philosophy and had fought the modernists ... and who had benefited research in the history of philosophy, and the renewal of educational programs" (*Storia d'Italia*, 320).

Croce would have liked the young generation to follow him and his philosophy, but they were more attracted to the new irrationalism that was sweeping Europe at the time: "a predatory spirit of conquest and adventure, violent and cynical" (*Storia d'Italia*, 321). For Croce, the age of pure poetry in Italy was over at the end of the previous century, and now both poetry and philosophy were silent. There was nothing for critics to comment on because the new poets, in trying to be modern, "self-destructed" by introducing elements in their work that disparaged it: "Artists leave very little to the critics to say because they carry on their own self-destructing analyses, and they fall in exaggerations or mannerisms, and, in order to be interesting, they make use of subjects and motives that are foreign to their very souls" (*Storia d'Italia*, 330). Croce has in mind mainly the works of Antonio Fogazzaro and Giovanni Pascoli; as for the works of the Futurists, "they are not even works of poetry, but of something else" (*Storia d'Italia*, 331).

If the young Italian intellectuals were attracted at first, even enthusiastic, when Croce's *Estetica* appeared in 1902, their enthusiasm was short lived. The irrationalism of the age seemed to be more attractive to them – though this was mostly true of those who called themselves Futurists and of those who joined their ranks – and Croce's work ceased to be of interest to them. The testimony of one of the brightest young minds, Renato Serra, illustrates this attitude and that of many young intellectuals of the time towards Croce, and also towards Gabriele D'Annunzio, the poetic icon for those who wanted to become poets, but whose star had also waned. In 1914, Serra wrote that for both Croce and D'Annunzio, who had dominated the fields of criticism and poetry respectively, their time had passed: "Today D'Annunzio and Croce are being placed aside" (Renato Serra, "Le lettere," 378). People still read them, they still follow them, but the signs of "weariness and of detachment are becoming visible." He describes this feeling as "a vague and subtle sense, not of hostility but of a well-established admiration of an already satisfied curiosity, which envelops the works of the two masters in a stifling museum-like air [una chiusa aria di museo]: the people go by their shop windows [to see], they know what is inside, they take a look and move on." There is a sense of an ending, that there is nothing new that one can expect from them, "that something is over, if not in these writers but in our conscience, that has already gone beyond them" (Serra, 379).

Of Croce in particular, Renato Serra reiterates the attitude of the new generation of critics and poets who find both Croce and D'Annunzio old-fashioned and antiquated: "[Benedetto Croce] rules with his persona over the field of criticism as D'Annunzio does over the field of poetry. We could go on with our comparison, since in both cases we are writing about an ending or, at least, an exhaustion, an overcoming

[superamento]; and here and there one hears of rebellion, of being bothered [fastidio], of almost a desire to do without [sottrarsi] a learning
[disciplina] that has had its day. A vain desire, in either case; a school-
boy's desire" (Serra, 452). Serra's chapter on Benedetto Croce is a fare-
well to someone who has by now done his work and has gone on his
way. Just as those who have completed a day's work and are now going
home, "so Croce; he has completed part of his work, and he has gone
away; his person is no longer part of the work of everyday, where it
seemed that we had him close to us as a companion, and he looms with
a profile that is no longer familiar." He asks whether Croce's work, in
the last ten or fifteen years, has achieved something great and lasting,
that man will preserve and will reflect on for years to come, or whether
it is just an ephemeral accomplishment, "a powerful and painstaking
labour, whose greatness dies with the worker" (Serra, 452).

The answer to this question is that Croce, to be sure, "was great for
us," and his work certainly dominated the thought of his generation,
but Serra wonders if the reasons are to be found in his greatness or
in their own shortcomings: "pochezza nostra, o vera grandezza sua?"
(Serra, 453). There is no easy answer, but, as Croce also intuited in *Storia
d'Italia*, he was among those who no longer spoke to the new generation, those who were by now "overcome" (i superati), those who no
longer spoke to the young generation of intellectuals who had either
outgrown them or simply wanted a change. For these young men and
for Serra, Croce had accomplished the best part of his work and no
longer mattered: "The Philosophy of Spirit is over; the *Critica* with volume XII, which was written a long time ago, ceases the battle (publication), and we could say that it is over; his important work on Vico is
done. What else is left for Croce to do?" (453). Serra lists all the work
that Croce has accomplished in the first series of his work and antici-
pates the work of the second series that he may do in the future, by
"emptying the drawer" of all the minor publications, "the analects,
the paralipomena" (453), that remain to be done, but he questions the
importance of this work and whether it is really being done for them
or for Croce himself: "it seems that all the things that Croce does now
are more important to him than to us" (454). At least, this is the impression that Croce gives to Serra and to the others, whether it is true or not.
Croce is not a creative genius in the sense that he is able to grasp an idea
and develop it, as Bergson does; Croce's intellect works in a "continu-
ous and dialectical progress" that flows evenly and undisturbed and is
not measured by the importance of the problems that he tackles; nor is

it exhausted in any one volume, because the nature of his progress is precisely that – "progress" (454). Croce is not so much a philosopher as he is an "activity" (attività), which is always alive, and "it can be more intense when it is most quiet and collected in modest terms" (455).

Serra comments on Croce's activity by summing it up as a "kind of certain facility and conventionalism of formulas, distinctions, and resolutions" that resolves every problem and every difficulty in the very act that they are proposed (Serra, 455). Alluding to his method of distinguishing and resolving errors in philosophy, as we have seen, in facile formulas of poetry and non-poetry, what is living and what is dead, this critical activity becomes exaggerated and mechanized in his followers, but also in Croce himself, for whom there are no problems in the universe that he cannot solve. For him it becomes almost a game that gives him the "honest pleasure of resolving them." The main issue, however, for Serra and for those of his generation is, what is the purpose of all this work? Is it for Croce's scholarly pleasure or to make a contribution to learning and to culture? Serra and the others feel left out, and Croce does not seem to be aware of their "impatience" or even of their "moral anguish" – as we saw from his account of this generation of poets and critics in *Storia d'Italia* – at his work that has become "a play of terms and formulas, so self-evident as to appear empty" (Serra, 455).

Serra's subtle critique is aimed at both Croce's critical method and his attitude towards the new generation. The help and advice that he gives to young intellectuals like Giovanni Papini, Antonio Borgese, and Giovanni Boine are really "lessons" (lezioni) that are mostly "unpleasant" and "one-sided" (chiuso), and more a "chastisement" (castigo) than an advice. Serra describes Croce as having an "indifferent impersonality" and as being "almost superficial in his liberality," as well as having something in him that is "closed, less reliable, in short, more distant" (Serra, 455). He criticizes him for his obsession with minute detail, with that "little thing" (una cosina) that still needs to be added to the philosophical edifice that he has already built, and with his tendency to take up already established conclusions and rework them over and over. One of his examples is the essay on the lyrical character of art, previously discussed, which for Serra is Croce's way of "progressing" (progredire) over his own formula that had been established in the *Estetica* of 1902. As for Croce's literary criticism, to Serra this is the least relevant of Croce's work: it appears to belong to the "old style rather than the new style" of literary criticism and gives the impression that the writer "has not read [his own]

Aesthetics" (457). It comprises essays of moral and literary psychology that focus more on the author and the content of the work than on the artist who is characterized by well-found formulas, such as saying that Carducci is the poet of history, and Pascoli the "poet-puer," and so on (456). In Serra's *Le Lettere* of 1914, Croce is no longer among the critics who are active and whose work creates interest. For him, Croce has already said everything, and what remains to be said are minor touches and retouches to an already established and completed system. The next generation of Italian intellectuals no longer expects to be surprised by new and exciting discoveries. Croce has said everything that he wanted to say, and now he is done.

Serra's assessment is to a certain extent close to the truth. Croce had by then written his best work, and there was little new that he would provide in the next years, which he mainly devoted to writing works of history and politics. Yet, Croce was not a "finished man" (uomo finito), because, as I have pointed out, what seemed to Serra and to others to be a pointless exercise of reworking old formulas was a critical preoccupation with the essential and important aspects of his philosophy that tormented him and that he always hoped to resolve, as in the essay on the lyrical character of art and in *La poesia*. In fact, it is precisely one of the aims of *A Croce Reader* to address and redress the perspective of critics like Renato Serra who, though well meaning, overlooked much of the importance of Croce's later work. One of these aspects, as I have indicated, is the essay on the lyrical character of art, which is the earliest attempt to void allegory and banish it from the realm of the aesthetic. The next attempt, in *La poesia*, is to place allegory in the category of literary expression. What appeared to Serra to be a useless exercise of reworking an already established philosophical system was, on the contrary, an attempt to limit the interference of allegory, to prevent it from invading (if not interfering with) philosophy, and to erase it. Croce's renaming of his philosophy as "absolute historicism" was equally an attempt in this direction to wed philosophy and history in order to keep philosophy alive.

Another aspect of Serra's comments that is worth discussing further is his remark that Croce's literary criticism seems to be written by someone who has never read the *Estetica*. This is certainly a very perceptive remark, though not entirely true. It is true, on the one hand, that Croce's analysis was always directed at a consideration of the content and of the man behind the work. On the other hand, Croce was always very keen to differentiate between what was poetic and what was not, which resulted from his attempt in the *Estetica* to distinguish what was poetic from what was prosaic, symbol from allegory. Nevertheless, it is a fact that in the ensuing years Croce did not have many followers who studied his philosophy, although he continued to be popular and to be read. So when a student from Turin, Aldo Mauti, wrote a thesis on his political philosophy, Croce was ecstatic. Gennaro Sasso, commenting on this episode of October 3, 1939, wrote that the news greatly comforted him, that a young man, "instead of insulting him, brought to the old thinker the concrete sign of [serious] study and meditation on his thought that he had accomplished with sincerity and passion." However, the comfort was short lived because, as Sasso relates, the young man died shortly afterwards (Sasso, 159).

The resistance to Croce and his philosophy was felt on every front well before and after his death. It took the form, in certain cases, of a "distance from Croce," as we have seen in the case of Renato Serra, but there is also another sense to this distance. Antonio Prete, a young and upcoming critic, in a work titled *La distanza da Croce* (The distance from Croce), claimed to measure Croce's distance from modern-day literary criticism and the avant-garde. At issue, for Prete, is not Croce's loyalty to an ethical conception of culture, his passion for liberty, his literary historiography, or his industrious organization of culture, but "the consistency of his myth" in his own time with respect to the avant-garde and to modern theories of literary criticism: "It is precisely on these grounds that the reasons for a distance from Croce are to be measured" (Prete, 59). The distance implies not an overcoming of Croce's philosophy but a reduction of our relation to Croce "to the zero degree" (al grado zero; Prete, 59). This reduction entails "a process of demystification" of his philosophy and, in particular, of his poetics and critical methodology (60).

Prete situates the ambiguity of Croce's myth in an aesthetics that, though providing "unknowingly" (inconsapevolmente) the justification for these avant-garde movements, later rejects them. Instead of acknowledging the movements as poetics, and their experimentalism as a "crisis of expressionism," Croce chose to define them as examples of irrationalism (as we have already seen) resulting from a "weakened and weary sense of distinction between truth and non-truth within the sphere of the theoretical" (*Storia d'Italia*, 253; quoted in Prete, 64). Thus, the avant-garde is relegated to the "extra-artistic ground of a neutral and indistinct irrationality" (Prete, 64). "Irrationalism," Prete writes, "is not so much an accusation as a respectable label employed to store the avant-garde in the attic of *non-poetry* and to justify his [Croce's] own aversion" (64). Croce's negative attitude towards the avant-garde is a measure of his broader relationship to contemporary literature and of his "mistrust" of the "new," which for him "is often nothing else but the will for the new, researched for its own sake and molded, however possible" (Croce, *Letture di poeti*, 324; quoted in Prete, 66). However, the spirit of the new is precisely the foundation of any avant-garde based on the "conscience, experimentation, and exasperation of the new" (Prete, 67). Croce's fear and mistrust of the new, for Prete, signals a mistrust of future advances in literary criticism, of "the broadening of a critical conscience," and of the "discovery of an artistic *function* within the complex articulation of the civilization of the image" (68). Croce's negative attitude is "another lesson in the ambiguity of his myth" since it clashes with the "constant lessons" of his key notion that all history is "contemporary" (69).

Prete's assessment provides us with an insight into the ways in which Italian critics like Prete sought a distance from Croce and espoused the new critical trends that were then popular on the European critical scene, such as structuralism and the semiotic analyses of Roland Barthes. Prete refers to these as "the names and the methods that for us young people are more eloquent than Croce's." He alludes to the new theories, popular at the time, of the "autonomy of the work of art" and, in critical method, of an emphasis on the symbol – "a reading and a re-invention of the symbolic apparatus" of the work (Prete, 75). He is in favour of a reading that consists of a line of criticism that is a continuation of the metaphors of the work – "not a paraphrase but a periphrasis" of the work; a reading that places emphasis on the notion of symbol that Croce seems to have denied with a theory and a practice that disregarded the symbol (as I have indicated, Croce understood the symbol as allegory). For Prete, the dangers facing the literary critic consist, precisely, in missing the symbolic character of the work (by which he did not mean *allegory*). Following Barthes, he warns that "the risk today is 'manquer le "symbole,"'" which can occur either by denying the reality of the symbolic level of the work in a reading that favours the literal or by privileging the symbolic to the extent that it turns into a sociological or psychoanalytic analysis (76).

The issue of the symbol is what determines the distance of Prete's generation from Croce's philosophy which, however, takes the form of a generational difference, of *old* versus *new*, but also of *middle class* versus *avant-garde*. From this critical perspective the distance from Croce becomes the distance from the middle-class values that the truth of his work exemplified: "the distance from the safety of the middle class with which criticism has often lived the truth of [Croce's] work" (Prete, 77).

From our perspective today, however, even the advanced criticism of Roland Barthes and his emphasis on the symbol belong to the past, superseded by other critics and other "–isms" that had not yet come on the scene when Prete wrote his essay. Does this imply that what comes later is always better than what comes before? Is critical distance to be measured in terms of the advancements that new literary trends seem to advocate over the old? Is a symbolic theory of art to be preferred to an allegorical one?

For the purpose of *A Croce Reader* the question becomes: from which Croce are we taking our distance? The answer is simple because neither Prete nor the Italian critics of his generation ever took into account the "other" Croce that we have discussed so far. The Croce against or from whom they always argued was a symbolic figure of their time and culture, not the critical Croce. Taking the distance from this latter Croce can only be done at one's peril – the peril of repeating the errors that Croce denounces and that he appears to resolve, but cannot. It could easily be shown that the insights of later critics have repeated, unknowingly, the same errors denounced by Croce, and that their critical insights could only be achieved by ignoring the rhetorical predicament denounced by Croce. The same can be said of the distance that contemporary literary criticism has taken from Croce today. The distance from Croce turns out to be the distance from an error that always passes for truth.

In so saying, we are not advocating a return to Croce. Croce himself discounted this possibility in an essay that anticipated such a return. If someone came on the scene, he wrote, wanting "to return to Croce," he (Croce) "from his icy marble tomb will praise and encourage his followers and critics not to go back but to always go forward, but with judgment [con juicio]" ("Necessità di tornare al De Sanctis," *Pagine Sparse*, vol. 3, 272–3). However, going forward does not mean embracing the avant-garde or new methods of literary criticism, as Prete and his generation of critics did. It implies continuing on one's path with a self-awareness of the errors to which any critical or philosophical system is subject – to go forward, yes, but *con juicio.*

In conclusion, to return to the task of the philosopher, as Croce defines it in the first essay of the *Anthology,* one would have to say that the obstacles that the philosopher dispels and disperses for the common man are obstacles that are not easily overcome, even by the philosopher. Whether the results are quick or slow to produce, they are never certain. However, this depends on which Croce we read. In Croce's *Anthology* the common man can certainly find the certainty that he or she is looking for and can experience the "divine" pleasure that the identity of knowing and doing guarantees, oblivious to the fact that the obstacles in the journey have not been removed or dispelled. Readers of *A Croce Reader*, however, will come to the realization that certainty in truth is only an illusion, that *intelligendo non fit omnia*, and that there is a fine line separating the meaninglessness and contradictions of myth and metaphysics and Croce's philosophy of absolute historicism. Readers will have to decide which Croce to read: whether to rethink Croce's philosophy in their own words or to sit like sceptics on the heap of the ruins of philosophy.

Massimo Verdicchio

A CROCE READER

Aesthetics

Aesthetics occupies a central role in Benedetto Croce's philosophy. The importance of aesthetics, long disregarded and reduced to a secondary role, becomes clear when we attempt to resolve many of the contradictions in his philosophy and mainly those related to aesthetics. These difficulties stem from an ambiguous conception of aesthetics that wavers between symbol and allegory. Following Hegel, Croce defines the concept of art as symbol, but when he defines representation and what determines artistic intuition, the examples point to allegory. In the first selection from the *Aesthetics* on imitation, the example of the coloured wax statues that imitate living beings, as in Madame Tussaud's wax museum, does not give us aesthetic intuition. However, if an artist paints a painting of the same coloured wax statues, we have artistic intuition. In this case our perception of the statues of coloured wax is mediated by the frame of the painting, which reveals that what we are looking at is art and not living beings. When representation and intuition are identical, that is, symbolic, we do not have artistic intuition, we do not have art; when intuition and representation are distinct, we have artistic intuition and allegory. The discrepancy between art as symbol and art as allegory, between statements and example, between sign and meaning, informs Croce's entire philosophical enterprise and determines the way we read his work. When we read it symbolically, it is possible to accept Croce's definition of philosophy as the identity of philosophy and history, or absolute historicism; when we read it allegorically, his philosophy is another metaphysics or myth. In the first case, we read how Croce wanted us to interpret him; in the latter case, we understand what he actually wrote.

In the *Estetica* of 1902, as well as in his other aesthetic works, Croce's critical methodology claims to separate symbol from allegory, poetry from prose, the poetic from the non-poetic or the prosaic. One of the first attempts is an essay titled "L'intuizione pura e il carattere lirico dell'arte" (Pure intuition and the lyrical character of Art; 1908), reprinted in *Problemi di Estetica* (1954), in which the lyrical character of art is said to be identical to pure intuition and separate from allegory. The next major separation can be found in *Storia dell'età barocca in Italia* (*History of the Baroque Age in Italy*; 1929), in which he associates allegory with both the beginning and the end of the Baroque age. It is only with *La poesia* of 1936 that Croce claims to have succeeded, finding a place for allegory under the category of literature. In the section included in *A Croce Reader*, "Literary Expression," the distinction between the poetic and the prosaic proves difficult to maintain, however, because it is impossible to determine where poetry ends and allegory begins. The example of Goethe's bird that is finally free but still retains the sign of its former captivity is a reminder of the indissoluble relation between symbol and allegory, poetry and prose, despite any attempt to separate them. The symbolic cannot exist separately from the allegorical, and it always retains the sign of its allegorical origins. Poetry can be conceived separately from allegory only in name and at the risk of being only a meaningless sign, an inscription, or a title on a book cover.

This apparent debacle is not a defeat but a victory. It is Croce's greatest contribution to aesthetics and to literary criticism – if not to philosophy. In his lifelong reflection on aesthetics and the struggle to distinguish the symbol from allegory, Croce shows that, despite his efforts, symbol and allegory are the two inseparable faces of art. If the symbol appears to be the essence of art, this is possible only in appearance and because allegory, which always resides in the margins, is what makes the symbol possible. As the third selection, "On the Nature of Allegory," makes clear, allegory is a form of writing, a cryptography, without which neither art nor philosophy is possible. The subtitle that Croce gave to the *Estetica* – *Come scienza dell'espressione e linguistica generale* (As science of expression and general linguistics) – points to the identity of language and aesthetics. Aesthetics is symbolic because language is symbolic. However, since the aesthetic is not the symbol but allegory, language is not a theory of the symbol but a theory of the sign. As Croce stated, between art and science, intuition and concept, there is a "dual" relation. There is intuition without concept, but not concept without intuition; there is allegory without symbol, but not symbol without allegory.

Art and Intuition

(*Aesthetics,* chap. 2, pp. 20–1)-

[20] The statement that art imitates nature is polysemous. With this claim truths have been asserted, or at least alluded to, and errors have been made, and most of the time nothing was meant at all. One of the more acceptable scientific meanings is when we understand by "imitation" a representation or intuition of nature, a form of knowledge. In this case, and to emphasize the spiritual character of the process, another statement is also legitimate: art is idealization, or imitation that idealizes nature. But, if by imitation of nature is meant that art provides mechanical reproductions, more or less perfect duplicates of natural objects, before which one feels the same commotion of feelings produced by natural objects, the statement is obviously wrong.

The painted wax statues that imitate living beings, and before which we remain astonished in museums of this kind, do not give us aesthetic intuition. Illusion and hallucination have nothing to do with the calm domain of artistic intuition. If an artist paints the scene of a wax museum, if an actor on stage portrays a man-statue in a farcical manner, we have once again the spiritual work and artistic intuition. Even photography is artistic to the extent that it communicates, at least in part, the intuition of the photographer, his point of view, the attitude and the situation that he made an effort to capture. And if photography is not entirely art, it is because the natural element cannot be entirely eliminated or subordinated. In fact, what photograph, even the most successful, gives us full satisfaction? What photograph would an artist not change, touch up, cut, or add to?

The claim, so often repeated, that art is not knowledge, that it does not provide truths, that it does not belong to the theoretical but to the sentimental world, is the consequence of not having recognized, precisely, the theoretical character of simple intuitions, which are distinct from both intellectual knowledge and perception, and of believing that the intellectual faculty alone – and, at best, perception – is knowledge. We saw that intuition is knowledge, free from concepts and simpler than the so-called perception of the real, and therefore that art is knowledge, is form, and does not belong to feelings and to psychic matter. If many thinkers of aesthetics insist on stressing that art is appearance [Schein], this is because they feel the need to differentiate it from the more complex act of perception, and to affirm it as pure intuition. And if we insisted that art is feeling, this was for the same reasons. In fact, once we exclude that the concept is the content of art, and once we exclude historical reality as such, there is no other content than reality captured merely in its ingenuity and immediacy, in its *élan vital* as feeling, that is, once again, as pure intuition.

Art and Philosophy
(*Aesthetics*, chap. 3, pp. 26–36, 39)

[26] The two forms of knowledge, aesthetic and intellectual or conceptual, are indeed different, but they are not separate or unrelated, as in two powers each pulling in a different direction. If we have shown that aesthetic form is completely independent from the intellectual and stands by itself without any external support, we did not say that the intellectual can stand without the aesthetic. This reciprocity would not be true.

What is the knowledge of concepts? It is the knowledge of relations of things, and things are intuitions. Without intuitions there are no concepts, just as without impressions intuitions are not possible either. Intuitions are this river, this lake, this brook, this rain, this glass of water. Concepts are water, not this or that appearance or that particular one, but water in general at any time and place it is realized. It is a matter of infinite intuitions but only of a single and constant concept.

However, if, on the one hand, the concept is the universal and no longer intuition, on the other hand it is intuition and it can only be intuition. Even the man who thinks, because he thinks, has impressions and feelings; his impressions and feelings will not be those of the non-philosopher, nor the love or the hate of certain objects and individuals, but they will be the very effort of thought, with the pain and the joy, the love and the hatred, that are related to it; hence the effort to become objective before the spirit can only take the form of intuition. To speak is not to think logically, but to think logically is also to speak. The fact that thought is inseparable from speech is a generally recognized fact. The negation of this thesis generates all sorts of errors and misunderstandings.

The first misunderstanding is had by those who believe that one can think equally with geometrical figures, algebraic signs, ideographs, without using speech, not even pronounced tacitly or almost imperceptibly within oneself; that there are languages in which the words, the phonic signs, do not express anything unless we also look at the written sign, and so on. But when we said "speech," we employed a synecdoche to mean, generically, "expression," which, as we noted, is not the only so-called verbal expression. Whether it is true that some concepts can be thought without any phonic representation, the examples we used to prove the opposite show that concepts are never without expressions […]

[28] What we can accept is that sometimes we have thoughts (concepts) in an intuitive form, an abbreviated expression, or, better, a peculiar one, sufficient for us but not enough to be easily communicated to another person or to more people. Thus, we say incorrectly that we have the thought but not the expression, when we should say, more properly, that we have the expression but it cannot be easily communicated yet. However, even this situation is relative and variable: there is always someone who grasps our thought right away and prefers it in that abbreviated form and would be annoyed if it were more developed, as is preferred by others. In other words, thought, logically and abstractly conceived, will be roughly the same, but aesthetically we are dealing with two different intuitions or expressions, in which different psychic elements enter each other. The same point can be made to destroy or to interpret correctly the entire empirical distinction between internal and external languages.

The highest manifestations, the peaks of intuitive and intellectual knowledge that shine from afar, are, as we know, Art and Science. Therefore, Art and Science are related and distinct at the same time; they coincide on one side, the aesthetic side. Every work of science is at the same time a work of art. The aesthetic side is hardly noticed when our mind is engaged in the effort of understanding the thought of the scientist and in examining his truth. But it becomes very noticeable when we pass from the activity of understanding to the contemplative one, and we see the thought unfold either transparent, clear, well defined, without any superfluous word, without inadequate words, with appropriate rhythm and tone, or confused, broken up, awkward, jumpy. Great thinkers are sometimes admired as great writers, whereas other thinkers, also great, remain more or less fragmentary writers, even though the fragments are harmonious, coherent, and perfect.

We forgive thinkers and scientists for being mediocre writers; the fragments, the moments of brilliance, compensate for the rest because it is easier to extract a well-ordered composition from the brilliant fragment, to release the flame from the spark, than to arrive at the brilliant discovery. But how can we forgive the pure artist for being a mediocre writer? "Neither gods nor men nor bookstalls have allowed mediocrity in poets" (Mediocribus esse poetis non dii, non homines, non concessere columnae) (Horace, *Ars Poetica*, Epist. 3.2, 373–4). The poet and the painter, if they lack form, they lack everything because they lack themselves. Poetry runs in the soul of everyone; only expression, that is, form, makes the poet. Here we find the truth of the thesis that denies art any content – by "content" meaning, precisely, the intellectual concept. In this sense, once we posit that the "content" is equal to the "concept," it is proper to state not only that art does not consist in content but also that it has no content.

Even the distinction between poetry and prose can be demonstrated in terms of the distinction between art and science. Since antiquity it has been understood that the distinction does not depend on external elements, such as rhythm and metre, blank verse and rhymed verse, but on internal ones. Poetry is the language of feeling, prose the language of the mind, but since the mind in its concreteness and reality is also feeling, every prose has its poetic side.

The relation between intuitive knowledge or expression and intellectual knowledge or concept, art and science, prose and poetry, can only be characterized as of double degree [doppio grado]. The first degree is the expression, the second the concept; the former can exist without the latter, but the latter cannot exist without the former. There is poetry without prose, but not prose without poetry. In fact, expression is the first declaration of human activity. Poetry is the "mother language of mankind"; the first men "were by nature sublime poets." This is also acknowledged in another way by those who observe that the shift from psyche to spirit, from animal sensation to human activity, is accomplished by means of language (but, they should say, of intuition or expression in general). It is not very precise to say, as is usually done, that language or expression is the intermediary link between the natural state and humanity, as if it were almost a mixture of the two. Where humanity appears the other has already disappeared. To be sure, by expressing himself, indeed, man leaves the natural state immediately. He leaves it. He is not half inside and half outside, as the image of the intermediary link would lead us to believe. Beside these two forms, the cognitive spirit knows no others. Intuition and concept exhaust it completely. The entire theoretical life of man takes place by passing from one to the other and in passing again from the second to the first.

History is inaccurately enumerated as a third theoretical form. This is not a form but a content; as form it is nothing more than intuition or an aesthetic fact. History neither looks for laws nor forms concepts; it neither induces nor deduces; it is directed *ad narrandum, non ad demonstrandum*; it does not construct universals or abstractions, but posits intuitions. The here and now, the *individuum omnimode determinatum*, is its dominion, just as it is the dominion of art. Therefore, history is reduced under the general concept of art [...]

[36] From these explanations it is clear that the pure or fundamental forms of knowledge are two: intuition and concept; Art and Science or Philosophy. They both reduce History into themselves, which is the result of placing intuition in contact with the concept, that is, when art, in receiving philosophical distinctions, remains nonetheless concrete and individual. All the others (natural sciences and mathematics) are impure forms: a combination of foreign and practical elements. Intuition gives us the world, the *phenomenon*; the concept gives us the *noumenon*, the Spirit [...]

[39] One of the errors to be corrected, or one of the ambiguities to be cleared up, is the notion that the essence of art is the symbol. But if the symbol is conceived as inseparable from artistic intuition, then it is synonymous with intuition, which has always an ideal character. Art does not have a double level [fondo], but only one, and everything in it is symbolic because everything is ideal. However, if the symbol is conceived separately, if on the one hand we express the symbol, and on the other the thing symbolized, we fall again into the intellectual error: the supposed symbol is the exposition of an abstract concept; it is allegory, it is science, or art that mimics science. But we should also be fair towards allegory and remark that in certain cases it is something entirely innocuous. Once Tasso had completed the *Gerusalemme liberata*, someone devised the allegory. Once Marino, the poet of lewdness, had completed the *Adone*, he suggested that the poem meant to show that "excessive pleasure ends in pain." To a statue of a beautiful woman the sculptor adds a sign stating that the statue represents "Mercy" or "Goodness." This allegory, which comes *post festum*, after the work has been completed, does not alter the work of art. So what is it? It is an expression added to another expression. To the poem *La Gerusalemme liberata* we add a page of prose that explains another thought of the poet. To the *Adone* a verse or a stanza is added that expresses what the poet would like some of his readers to know. To the statue only a word is added: "Mercy" or "Goodness."

Literary Expression

(*La poesia*, pt. 1, chap. 6, pp. 42–50)

[42] In the survey we conducted of the forms of spiritual life and their corresponding expressions we did not encounter the literary expression that clearly is neither poetry nor prose; it is neither the oratory expression nor the sentimental nor the passionate expression. In truth, it was impossible to encounter it because literary expression belongs to another spiritual level and not to these fundamental forms. In fact, it is possible to know and to function without necessarily having to pass by literature, or by the "belles lettres" [bella letteratura] as it was once called. Ancient orators admitted as much when, with Cicero, they acknowledged that history can be written "sine ullis ornamentis" (without any ornamentation), as chroniclers used to do, as long as they "intelligatur quid dicat" (meant what they said), and, of course, "sine mendacio" (without lying), and that is why historians, as long as they are mere historians, are "non exornatores sed tantummodo narratores" (not embellishers but only narrators); or that from philosophy and science we do not require the "ornatus" (embellishment); or when, as we indicated, they agreed with Quintilian on the effectiveness of persuasion even without the word.

Literary expression originates from a particular act of spiritual economy, which is represented in a particular disposition and institution. It must be taken into account that spiritual moments, the forms of the spirit, though indivisible in their concreteness, are specific in the single individual not because of an abstract division but because of a sort of greater energy or prevalence and because of habit and conformity to virtue. Hence we have the division of the single man into man of action, into contemplative man, into poet and philosopher, into naturalist and mathematician, into politician and clergy, and so on for all the more particular specifications that are not necessary to list or to give as examples here. This is necessary for the work of art, and therefore it is permitted and willed by single men, by humanity, but one must be on guard [vigilando] against specifications that are perverted by separation and reciprocal indifference, which would entail the disintegration of the spirit and of specification itself, and against specialists becoming *dimidiati viri*, no longer whole men. By spiritual economy is meant maintaining the balance between specifications so that they are all collected together not only in society but in the individual, and so that they all remain present and active. We call the former *civilization* and the latter *education* in its harmonious and universal characters, which is what we call *culture*. And since the disruption in the calm and normal flow of everyday life, of great changes and progress, of great actions and works does not occur without some greater or lesser degree of imbalance in the social forces and without inevitable destructions, those actions and events always have something revolutionary, violent, or even barbaric about them. And since in individuals the absorption of an idea, a mission, an artwork brings about a similar imbalance and almost a semblance of obsession and mania, the expression was forged that *"nullum grande ingenium est sine mixtura dementiae"* [no great genius is without some degree of madness], which, when translated in terms of naive positivism, became the theory that "genius is madness," with the inevitable opposite conclusion that madmen have genius.

Literary expression is part of civilization and education, similar to courtesy and etiquette, and consists of the established harmony between non-poetic expressions (passionate, prosaic, rhetorical, or persuasive) and those poetic ones in such a way that the former in their course, without denying themselves, do not offend poetic and artistic conscience. Therefore, if poetry is the mother language of mankind, literature is its governess in civilization, or at least one of them appointed to that end. The song of poetry also rises in coarse and rural periods; in fact, there are those who believe, exaggeratedly, that the only favourable social condition for poetry is barbarism. However, literature does not thrive in those times, otherwise they would have reached with it the opposite condition of civilized.

The balance between the two orders of expression is attained not by sacrificing one to the other, in a subordination that is excluded even here, but by taking both into account, and their tempering in the new form of expression, which is practical or conceptual or sentimental at certain moments, and poetic in another. A poetics of poetry that takes on those extrapoetic motives as its premises, respecting them for what they are. So that a "love story" provides the "intellect" ["ingegno"] to attest to that love ornately [bellamente] (*"ingenium nobis ipsa puella facit"*), and in poetry one looks for the way to reach the beloved's heart (*"ad dominam faciles aditus per carmina quaero"*), and an indignation, an "indignatio," that trembles in the breast against everything that should not be in man and in society, "becoming verse" (*"facit* versus"). Let's call them beautiful and robust "verses" but not intuition, contemplation, rapture, and ecstasy because in that case those motives would vanish and be resolved in something else: verses and similar ways of speaking well and ornately, namely, form that is distinguished from the content and which is only the "dress" of the content. [...]

[45] Ever since my first inquiries and investigations into the science of aesthetics I have refuted and expelled from its sphere the concept of form as "dress," of beauty as "ornament" [ornato], which is added to the "naked" expression by demonstrating it to be contradictory and absurd. To demonstrate this absurdity I indicated the dual expedient of a "convenient" [addition] that was used to provide a remedy that did not originate from within the form itself. And I was certainly correct in all this because that concept of a practical application to satisfy two different requirements was poorly transferred by writers of Rhetoric and Poetics, of aesthetics and criticism, and placed in the other poetic form, defacing and corrupting its nature. But in my still youthful radicalism I did not ask if there was another place in which what was intolerable in poetry was no longer intolerable; a place that had to exist, otherwise the error would have never existed, because error is generated by transferring one order of concepts to another, different one. By rectifying my youthful radicalism, as I have always tried to do in every part of my work and life, I have discovered that place that is none other than "literary expression."

Just as the concept of form varies in the sphere of literature, the meaning of the word "beauty" also changes. It no longer refers to the goddess who inspires a sense of both pleasure and pain as in Euripides' definition of Love, but rather to a gentle and respectable person who alleviates and refines the impulse of others and interprets it with a calm and harmonious voice. The concept of art also changes and is no longer identical to the poetic formulation of the expression, but differs from it as elaboration of literary expression, so much so that "art" and "poetry" sometimes even oppose each other. The concept of taste also changes and is no longer the conscience of poetry that makes itself and watches over itself in its process; it is something that is practical and that, better than others, characterizes the attributes of "reason" and "reasonableness" necessary to practice; it is called "taste," but it can also be called "tact" [tatto]. Furthermore, with this shift between poetic and practical faculties the concept of taste first made its appearance as a doctrine in the seventeenth century with Italian critics and writers of treatises and with the Spaniard Baltasar Gracián. The concept of "genius" also changes by taking the other name that has a similar etymology, "ingenium" or "wit," which also suggests more directly the practical act of devising [congegnare]. The same abandonment that was so dear to poetry and was its unfailing sign, the abandonment to the universal, is no longer necessary; on the contrary, it is important to always have the appointed goal clear and never lose sight of it, and never lose sight of the men whom one is addressing, the specific audience. The "sacred fury," the "divine mania," the "inspiration" of genius are foreign to literature and would not be of any use to it. However, what is not foreign to it is the other type of inspiration, which is the serious readiness for having things to say, the fondness for thought, for action, for the feeling that is ours and that also requires warmth and spontaneity: the gift of writing [scriver di vena]. And yet, not even literary expression, though opposite to poetry and related to practice, becomes craft [mestiere], because if the conviction fails, that is, its sincerity, it becomes empty and therefore cold, forced, grating, and bombastic; in short, it becomes bad literature. While mediocre artists are probably better paid than most, they are always despised. That conviction for things to say that takes over the soul is embodied in "style," a concept more properly literary because in literature there are as many styles as there are individuals and things (hence the debate about whether style is the "man" or the "thing"); whereas in poetry, however infinitely varied, style is only one, namely, the eternal and unmistakable sign of poetry, which echoes throughout the ages and places and in the most diverse subjects.

Kant had a glimpse of the nature of literature or rhetoric ("*Beredsamkeit*"), as it is also known, when he said that it is "the art of treating a matter of the intellect as a free play of the imagination" – an incomplete definition, however, made worse by the analogical and antithetical definition of poetry that follows it: "a play of the imagination treated as a matter of the intellect." Baumgarten was more direct in qualifying the "*representationes oratorie*" as "*imperfectae*" compared to poetry's "*repraesentatio perfecta.*" However, he did not develop the positive determinations hidden in the negative character of the imperfections, the limitations that literary expressions have in their realistic motives, which in limiting them are in turn limited by them. The reciprocal limitations and the inseparability of the two moments make it impossible to ever take literary form separately and to enjoy it as poetry because in every word, in every position, in every rhythm, in every inflection the form reveals the presence of the realistic motive, and the convenience lies in this relation.

When we read Cicero's *Against Verres II* where he magnificently expounds on the many thoughts and affections, memories and hopes, that the citizens of ancient and glorious Segesta attached to the artistically perfect statue of the goddess Diana, which had stood in their town, that the victorious Carthaginians had taken to Carthage, and that victorious Scipio had brought back, to their great joy, and placed on a high pedestal – the virgin goddess with arrows over her shoulders, the bow in her left hand, and a torch in her right – as well as the agony and the weeping that had accompanied its departure when Verres had stolen it, we have all the material for a historical ballad arranged by Platen. But Cicero did not write a ballad, and those pages retain in each and every part the imprint of the prosecuting lawyer who wrote it. When we read the famous pages from Cicero's *Pro Archia* where with very moving words he celebrates the incomparable benefits that come from [classical] studies, the company that books bring, how they temper the spirit against the vicissitudes of Fortune: pages that seem to be lyrical and yet are not lyrical. These expressions, even though they soar [lyrically], are like the bird in Goethe's poem that, having broken the thread, flies for the countryside, but it is not the bird that it once was because it now carries a small thread attached to its leg: a sign that once it belonged to someone. About books of literature, history, philosophy, or autobiography we usually say that "it reads like a novel," "it seems like a play," but these are exaggerated claims that are made moderate and brought down to earth by those "seems" and "like."

Similarly to rhetoric, literature has had its detractors. First of all, among practical men who aim straight at their purpose without qualms or who trample on any aesthetic consideration, or "flowery ornament," as the jeering expression goes; and also among the sufferers who are in love, or are otherwise passionate and restless but are unable to free themselves from the grip of their passion, and it seems to them sometimes that they violate its sincerity if they take their time in looking for beautiful words to express it. Finally, its detractors are among thinkers and scientists who are prickly and asocial enemies of the Graces. Other readers prefer extra-literary expressions to literature, and therefore they like frenzied rhetoric, disorderly expressions, scientific sketches, unadorned pages, finding them to be closer to lived reality. But these belong to the researchers of historical documents for whom, as is natural, overlapping literary formulations are only a hindrance [...]

[49] However, as we all know, literature can defend itself by the very fact that it continues to be read throughout the civilized world. In the Western world it has been appreciated ever since the Sicilians Corax, Tisias, and Gorgias opened schools [of rhetoric] and began to teach it in precepts and doctrines. The tradition continued even in the Middle

Ages in scattered cultural centres, which seem to have been more interested in literature and rhetoric than in poetry, until we arrive at the Humanists of the Renaissance and post-Renaissance, which was the great age of literature and of men of letters. Even in the last centuries, rationalism and enlightenment notwithstanding, which looked for things and not for words, and Romanticism that preferred moans, screams, and frenzy but not studied and composed expressions and gave therefore a bad reputation to the expression *"ars rhetorica,"* and despite the lack of subtlety and urbanity of our present age, the virtue of literary decorum exists and works, even if in a limited sphere, and contributes, as it can, to preserve the forms of civilization.

But poetry is not one of literature's enemies, which it accompanies as the inferior companion that does not reach its height, and does not even try to stand up to it, because in doing so it would sign its own death warrant. What better companionship would suit it? Under the spontaneous guise of the "written arts" or "literary institutions" we have always dealt with the theory of poetry together with the theory of literature under the name of "history of literature" or "history of poetry and rhetoric," narrating their two stories together. Aristotle observed that we lacked a common name for both, but we will never be able to find the name because poetry and literature, though sharing a common side, remain two different things.

On the Nature of Allegory

(*Nuovi saggi di estetica*, pp. 331–8)

[331] To state that allegory is an expression similar to others means that it is one of the many forms classified by Rhetoric and that we still use it in schools today. All of them are subject to philosophical scrutiny, which reduces them from abstract to concrete and resolves them, as is well known, in the infinite individualization of the sole poetic form. Well, this is the crux: whether allegory is or is not a form of expression – and I was under the illusion that I had shown that, in fact, allegory is not a form of expression.

Those who are not inexperienced or unmindful of literary things should have a vague sense of this truth, besides a clear and distinct idea, or a premonition, remembering and observing the loathing of which allegory has always been made the object in aesthetics and in modern literary criticism. A loathing that, to my knowledge, no one has ever felt either for metonymy or for apostrophe, or hypotyposis – in short, for any of the other figures of speech or rhetorical tropes. Hegel used to call it icy and bleak (*frostig und kahl*), a product of the intellect and not of concrete intuition and of the deep feeling of imagination, and lacking inherent seriousness, prosaic, and distant from art (*Vorlesung über Aesthetik*, I, 499–501). Vischer saw in allegory the complete dissolution of the original relation between idea and image. He believed it to be a sign of either artistic decline or artistic immaturity, he denounced its non-organic character, and he satirized it as being enveloped in mystery (*Geheimnissthuerei*) but not deep in mystery (*Geheimniss*) (*Aesthetik*, II, 467–71). I will not indulge in quotations; I will limit myself to quoting Francesco De Sanctis's constant polemics against allegory – "Allegorical poetry is boring poetry" – and its kin – "Political poetry is bad poetry."

To be sure there is also an allegory in the rhetorical sense and of which Quintilian and other ancient and modern rhetoricians speak, such as De Colonia and Blair, namely, allegory as inversion, as Quintilian puts it, that "*aut aliud verbis, aliud sensu ostendit, aut etiam interim contrarium*" (presents one thing by its words and either a different or sometimes even a contrary thing by its sense) (and in the latter case it takes the name of irony) (*Institutio Oratoria*, VIII, 6, 44; Loeb trans.); or as prolonged metaphor, as Blair defined it (*Lectures on Rhetoric and Belles Lettres*, London, 1823, 158–9). Allegory with this meaning can be found in that passage from Cicero, "*Equidem cetera temptestates et procellas in illis dumtaxat fluctibus contionum semper Miloni putavi esse subendas*" (I thought that Milo would always have other storms and squalls to weather, I mean in the troubled waves of our public assemblies) (Quintilian 8.6.48; Loeb trans.); or in Terence, "*Suo sibi gladio hunc iugulo*" (I am killing him with his own sword) (Terence, Ad. 958) (See R. Volkmann, *Die Rhetorik der Grichen und Römer*, Leipzig, 1885, 429–33) ; or to mention an entire composition, Horace's ode to the ship, which is a simple emotional poetic fantasy. But this allegory in the rhetorical sense, which rhetoricians in general try to differentiate empirically from "similitude" or from "metaphor," is not the same one that created difficulty for Dante and other poets. It is not the one that generates the loathing of aesthetics and of modern criticism, and, finally, it is not the one that needs a special investigation and a special scientific concept. [...]

[335] For these reasons it seemed to me essential not to restrict myself to a mere negation and rejection of allegory but to proceed by better determining it by itself, positively, in its own function. This way one

could shed light on the essential heterogeneity of allegory towards art, glimpsed and asserted rather than demonstrated. Therefore, I defined allegory (and I believe I was the first) as a practical act, a type of writing (because writing is something practical), a cryptography, not essentially different from any cryptography even if, instead of letters or numbers, one uses spoken or illustrated images. From this definition I derived the laws of allegory, and I explained why, where the authentic interpretation or the author's statements are lacking, where a good cryptographic system is lacking with its relative key, deciphering allegorical works is a hopeless task, constantly hypothetical, and, at best, only capable of aspiring to some greater or minor degree of probability. [...]

[337] Actually what happens, as I have said elsewhere, is that either the poet forgets the intentional world for the fantastic world and surrenders to poetic inspiration (unless later he comments on it allegorically), or he interferes continuously in his fantastic world with his intentional world and disrupts the aesthetic coherence of the work, producing a whole that is not poetry and has value only as cryptography … (I remark here in parentheses that the same is the case with historiography where a perfectly critical historical account can be allegorized by applying a cautionary ending, generally rhetorical, and in this case the historical work remains uncontaminated; or that aim can penetrate the work, altering it, and we get a tendentious historiography that is no longer history but rhetoric. And even here the intermediate cases are many.)

All this confirms my conclusion that the critic must focus solely on rejecting this allegory that wants to take the place of poetry, as one rejects any other poetic vacuity or ugliness. In general, one does not need to bother about allegorical interpretation, because where one considers allegory, one does not consider poetry, and vice versa. In Dante's case, because he is one of the greatest poets of humanity, allegory is almost always extrinsic and only very rarely does it interfere with the poetry; if it appears to do so frequently, if not continuously, the commentators are to blame who have burdened with allegories what is in fact lofty poetry.

The interpretation of allegories, the reading of cryptograms, is a completely different type of inquiry, and it is extraneous to criticism. This is something that delights or worries many people, or at least many Dante scholars. I have never denied nor will I deny now out of spite that this type of inquiry, when there are the conditions for arriving at a certain degree of probability, has its own share of curiosity. I am reminded, in this context, of the beginning of the *Phaedrus* when Socrates, forced to speak on the myth of Boreas and Orithyia, after listing the naturalist explanations that have been given by clever men, declares that on his part he refuses to engage in these clever speculations because, he says, "if I were to do that, I would have to explain also the appearance of Centaurs, Chimaeras, Gorgons, and Pegasuses, but it would take me too much time, and there would not be time to fulfil the Delphic oracle to know myself, the Typhons and all the other benign and mad forms that are myself." As far as I am concerned, I leave those inquiries and debates to those who have time to waste or, to say it with Dante, to those who, knowing very little, are not worried about wasting time.

Philosophy

This section contains excerpts from Croce's *Logic*, his reading of Hegel, and his reading of G.B. Vico. The three essays are different in nature, yet they have a common theme. The selection from the *Logic* deals with the identity of history and philosophy. In an essay of 1893, "La storia ridotta sotto il concetto generale dell'arte" (History reduced under the general concept of art), Croce associates history with art and groups it under the general concept of art. We find the same claim in the *Estetica* of 1902, as we have seen in the section on aesthetics. However, in the *Logic* he claims not only that history should be grouped with philosophy but also that history and philosophy are identical. This perception results from a new understanding of philosophy and history as concrete and no longer as abstract sciences, which makes their identity possible. The implications of this shift are critical for the later developments of Croce's philosophy of the Spirit, which becomes a philosophy of absolute historicism, as it is made more explicit in the section on history. The essay on Hegel that bears the polemical title of "What Is Living and What Is Dead in Hegel's Philosophy" exemplifies Croce's historico-critical method of doing philosophy, which is to separate pure or living philosophy from empirical, non-philosophical elements, or dead philosophy. Croce's reading of Vico's *New Science* attempts a similar distinction by separating the philosophical gold from the empirical dross with which it is joined and con-fused, namely, by dividing good philosophy from error, symbol from allegory. Croce's critical method of doing philosophy is not different from the method he employs in the *Aesthetics* of 1902, where he separates the symbol from allegory, or in *La poesia*, where he distinguishes poetry from literature, and poetry from prose. Hegel's error of taking distinct concepts for dialectical ones, and Vico's error of confusing empiricism with philosophy, are the result of rhetorical or metaphorical interference in the discourse of philosophy, that is, of an arbitrary element that introduces itself into thought and subverts it. The disruption of the conceptual is a constant in Croce's philosophical system and characterizes the impossibility of drawing a firm line between intuition and concept or, at the level of representation, between symbol and allegory. Croce warns the reader to be on guard against these interferences and to always reassess his or her position if necessary. He also warns the reader to always be careful when reading philosophy because this awareness may make all the difference between philosophy and metaphysics, pure philosophy and an allegory of philosophy. This is the burden of Croce's philosophy – but also his greatest insight.

The Identity of Philosophy and History
(*Logic*, pp. 223–35)

[223] Now that the conditional character of philosophy for history has been established, it is necessary to determine, just as clearly, the conditional character of history for philosophy. If history is not possible without the logical or philosophical element, philosophy is not possible without the intuitive or historical element.

A philosophical proposition, or definition, or system (as we called it) is born in the mind of a given individual, at a determined point in time and space, and in determined conditions, and therefore it is always historically conditioned. Without the historical conditions that posit the question, the system would not be what it is. Kant's philosophy could not have been written at the time of Pericles, because it presupposes, at least, the exact science of nature that was developed from the Renaissance onwards, as this depended on geographical discoveries, industrialization, capitalism or the rise of the middle class, and so on. It also presupposes the scepticism of David Hume, who in turn presupposes the deism of the early-eighteenth century, which in turn goes back to the religious wars of England and Europe in the sixteenth and seventeenth centuries, and so on. However, if Kant had lived in our time, he could not have written the *Critique of Pure Reason* without modifying it so radically that it would be not only a new book but a new philosophy, even though it included his old philosophy.

In the obstinacy of his old age Kant rejected Fichte's interpretations and advancements and ignored Schelling's, but he could not ignore either Hegel or Schleiermacher, or Herbart, or even Schopenhauer – in fact, not even the representatives of speculative philosophy of the Middle Ages, who followed the classical period of modern philosophy: the authors of positivist myths, the Kantian and Hegelian schools, the new combinations of Platonism and Aristotelianism, that is, of pre-Kantian and post-Kantian philosophy, the new sophists and sceptics, the new Plotinus school and mystics, and the moods and the events that conditioned all these things.

After all, Kant lives again in our time with a different name (and what is the individual marked by a name if not a mishmash of syllables?), and he is the philosopher of our time, in whom that philosophical thought continues that at one time took the name, among others, of the Scottish-German name of "Kant." The philosopher of our time, whether he wants to or not, cannot jump out of the historical conditions in which he lives, or pretend that what happened before him did not happen. Those events are in his bones, in his flesh, and in his blood, and he must account for them, that is, he must know them historically. And the breadth of his philosophical knowledge will vary to the extent of his historical knowledge. If he did not know those events and only brought them within him as simple facts, he would not be different from an animal (or from ourselves as animals, as beings who are – or, rather, seem – entirely immersed in will and in practice). The animal, in fact, is conditioned by all of nature and by all of history but does not know it. It is necessary therefore, to arrive at the truth of the answer, that one understands the meaning of the question, and, for the truth of philosophy, that one knows history.

[226] By changing history, philosophy changes too, and because history changes at every instant, philosophy is new at every instant. We can observe this in the case of the communication of philosophy from one individual to another by means of the oral or the written word. Even in that transmission the change occurs quickly because when we have remade simply in ourselves the thought of a philosopher, we are in the same conditions of those who have appreciated a sonnet or a melody and have adjusted their spirit to that of the poet or the composer, but this is not satisfactory in philosophy. We can remain ecstatic in reciting a poem and in executing a piece of music without altering it in any way, but we do not seem to own a philosophic proposition unless we translate it, as they say, into our own language, when on its

bases we form new philosophical propositions and resolve new problems that have surged within us. That is why no one book satisfies us
entirely but only quenches our thirst to make us thirsty for another. So
much so that when we have finished reading, or while we are reading,
we often regret not being able to dialogue with the author, and we have
the tendency, as did Socrates in the *Phaedrus*, to judge written speeches
as if they were paintings because they do not reply to our questions but
they always repeat what they say (*Phaedrus*, 275). Or we can become
impatient like that professor from Padua in the fifteenth century who,
in commenting on the jurist Paul and annoyed by the difficulties he had
encountered, cried out, "This damned Paul speaks so obscurely that
if I had him in my hands, I would seize him by the hair and question
him." But if, instead of the silent book, we had the living man, and we
grabbed him by the hair and forced him to speak clearly, the outcome
would be the same: his words would be translated into ours; his problems would arouse within us our own problems [...]

[232] Philosophy is neither outside, nor on top, nor at the end; nor is
it achieved in a moment or at some particular moment in history, but
it is obtained in every moment, and it is always and entirely tied to the
course of events and conditioned by historical knowledge. Nonetheless, this conclusion to which we have arrived and which fully corrobo-
rates with the other about the conditionality of philosophy for history
must still be held to be provisional. If we were to consider it definitive, philosophy and history would be for us two forms of the spirit
that condition each other reciprocally or, in a not-so-happy formula, in
reciprocal action. Philosophy and history are not two forms, but only
one form, and they do not condition one another; in fact, they identify
with one another. The a priori synthesis that is the concreteness of individual judgment and of definition is, at the same time, the concreteness
of philosophy and of history. Thought, by creating itself, qualifies intuition and creates history. Neither does history precede philosophy, nor
does philosophy precede history; each is born at one birth. Any priority
or primacy that can be accorded to philosophy can only be made in the
sense that the sole form, philosophy-history, takes its characteristic, and
therefore deserves the name, not from intuition but from what transfig-
ures intuition: thought and philosophy.

For didactic purposes, philosophy and history are distinct when we
consider philosophy as that form of exposition that emphasizes the
concept or system, and history as that form that emphasizes individual
judgment or narrative. But since every narrative includes the concept,

every narrative serves to clarify and resolve philosophical problems, and, vice versa, every conceptual system throws light on facts. Hence, the confirmation of the effectiveness of the system is in the power that it demonstrates in interpreting and narrating history: history is the touchstone of philosophy. Their close unity is clear when one examines closely a philosophical and a historical proposition, even though the two may appear different because of their extrinsic and literary differences with which they are treated in writings or in books, and even though their didactic division relies on different dispositions that the exercise in turn contributes to determine, their close unity becomes clearer as long as one goes to the bottom of either a philosophical proposition or a historical one. The contrast often mentioned between philosophy and history is really between two philosophies, one true and the other false, or both partly true and partly false. If someone, for instance, is an idealist in writing history and a materialist in theory, it means that in his spirit, without being aware of it, two non-harmonized philosophies coexist. Doesn't it happen often that in the same philosophical exposition one finds propositions that contradict each other and diverging systems arbitrarily thrown together?

From intuition, which is indiscriminate individualization, we move to the universal, which is discriminate individualization, and from art to philosophy, which is history. The second degree, precisely because it is second, is more complex than the first, but this complexity does not imply that it is broken into minor degrees, philosophy and history. The concept, in a single stroke [colpo d'ala], asserts itself and takes possession of the entire reality, which is not different from the concept but is the concept itself.

Note

Allow me to clarify something that concerns the history and the related critique of my own thinking. Sixteen years ago I made my debut in philosophy with an essay titled "History reduced under the general concept of Art" [La storia ridotta sotto il concetto generale dell'Arte, 1893], in which I claimed not just that history is art (as the title indicates) but that history can be reduced under the general concept of Art. After sixteen years I am now claiming instead that history is philosophy, in fact that history and philosophy are the same thing. The two theories are certainly different, but a lot less than they may appear to be. And, in any case, the latter is the unfolding and the perfecting of the first.

Elle a bien changé sur la route without doubt, but it has changed without discontinuities and leaps. In fact, my intentions in the youthful study were first of all to fight the attempt by the natural sciences, then more than now, to resolve history within their system; second, to assert the theoretical character of art and its seriousness that the then-dominant positivism considered a thing of pleasure; and, third, to deny that historicity constituted a third form of the theoretical spirit, different from the aesthetic and conceptual forms. Even now I have kept these three theses just as they were, and they have become part of my *Aesthetics* and my *Logic.* However, at that time the proper character of philosophy was not clear to me, which was deeply different from the empirical and abstract sciences; nor was the difference between philosophical Logic and classifying Logic clear. Because of this shortcoming I could not completely resolve the problem that I had set myself. By confusing in one group, then, the true universality of philosophy and the false universality of the sciences (which is mere universality or abstraction), it seemed to me that the concreteness of history could only be grouped with art, understood in its general sense; that is why I wrote "general concept of art" and characterized it by the erroneous method of subordination and co-ordination, as representation of the real, placing it without mediation next to the representation of the possible, that is, art in the strict sense. When in the progress of my thinking (a slow and difficult progress because slow and difficult it was for men of my generation to reacquire the conscience of what is really philosophy) I understood the true relation of philosophy and the sciences, and I freed myself at the same time from the scoriae of the intellectualistic and naturalistic methods, I came to understand the true nature of history. In the *Aesthetic* I regarded it as originating from the intersection of philosophy and art; in the *Outline of Logic* [*Lineamenti di Logica*] I took a step forward, and history seemed to me the conclusion of the theoretical spirit, the sea in which the river of art flows, enlarged by the river of philosophy. However, the identity of history and philosophy was still hidden from me because I still held on to the prejudice that philosophy, somehow, could not be bound by history and could not constitute, with respect to it, either a previous or an independent moment of the spirit. That is to say, in my idea of philosophy still persisted something abstract, but even this prejudice and this abstraction were slowly overcome. I was helped in this not only by my studies on the *Philosophy of Practice* and the relation of identity that I discovered between intention and action but also, and above all, by the work of my very good friend Giovanni Gentile (who has been a great

help and stimulus to my mental life) on the relation between philosophy and the history of philosophy (see *Critica*, VII, pp. 142–9), which I
extended in general to the relation of philosophy and history. In short,
by emphasizing the concrete character that history has with respect
to the empirical and abstract sciences, I have moved on, gradually, to
emphasize the concrete character of philosophy. After I had brought
to completion the critique of the double abstractions, the two concrete
ones (the one that I first claimed for history and later for philosophy)
proved themselves to be only one. Thus I could no longer entirely accept
or reject my old theory, which is not the new one but is closely related
to it. This was the process that I underwent, and I wanted to describe it
on purpose in order not to leave any misunderstandings that, because
of my negligence, could have led others to error.

The Relation of Distincts and the False
Application of the Dialectic
(Saggio sullo Hegel, chap. 4, pp. 53–66)

[53] How did it happen that this philosophical thought, which was
established with so much logical depth, rich with powerful truths,
harmonious and friendly towards concreteness, passion, imagination,
and history, appears to be instead abstract, intellectualistic, arbitrary,
and contrived, opposed to history, to nature, and to poetry – in short,
the opposite of what it wanted to be? How can we explain the violent
reaction against it, which seemed lucky and definitive, and that only
very light minds (and not very Hegelian) could explain, and only with
fortuitous reasons, with unintelligence and ignorance? On the other
hand, why *that* philosophical thought was invoked to help many of
the most diverse orientations, especially, from those that Hegel had
meant to fight and overcome, chiefly materialism and theism? And
why, for instance (if I am allowed a personal memory that alludes to
an event that is not merely personal), I, who write and has interpreted
and commented on the Hegelian doctrine of the synthesis of opposites
for many years of my intellectual life, now feel a strong reluctance to
Hegel's system, especially the one presented in the *Encyclopedia* with
the subdivision of Logic, Philosophy of Nature, and Philosophy of the
Spirit, and which Hegelians show off and recommend? And why is it
that in rereading those works I feel rising within me the old aversion?
We must find the underlying reasons for all this, after having outlined

the healthy part of the system to reveal the diseased part. After having shown what is living in Hegel's system to show what is dead, namely, what is left unburied and still hinders the very life of what is living.

We should not be too accommodating and contented with making a concession that has often been offered by the Hegelians of strict observance and by whom it was acknowledged that Hegel could have erred and did err in many statements on questions of history, natural sciences, and mathematics, as well as on the state of the epistemology of his own time and on the limitations of his own individual culture; that is why this part of the system should be re-examined and corrected, or even be entirely redone, keeping in mind the progress made in these fields in the last few years. In other words, only Hegel the historian and the naturalist is lacking and outdated, which means that the philosopher who does not base his truths on empirical data remains intact.

His opponents are not satisfied with making this concession, and rightly so because what creates aversion to Hegel's system is not the quality or the quantity of the erudition it contains (highly admirable despite the shortcomings and what appears to be outdated), but rather his philosophy, in fact. Earlier I did not want to account for the effectiveness of Hegel's thought on historical studies as something detached and independent from the very principles of the system. For these same reasons I am not prepared to consider how the origin of his errors is independent from his philosophical principles. Those errors that appeared to be historical and naturalistic are, in fact and for the most part, philosophical errors because they are determined by his thinking, by his way of conceiving history and the science of nature. Hegel is thoroughly honest, and it is to his honour that his errors on the whole cannot be explained as a fortuitous encounter of incoherence and distraction.

Therefore, the problem is to find the philosophical error or errors (or the fundamental one and the others that derived from it) that combined and mixed in Hegel's mind with his immortal discovery, and which justifies our reaction against the Hegelian system, against that aspect to which the reaction was not the usual obstacle encountered by all original truths, but it presented an obvious character of reasonableness. And since, in conformity to what has already been remarked, the logic of philosophy formed the main area of Hegel's mental activity, one can assume that the origin of the error is there, which in that case would be an error in logical theory ... [55] As a result, Hegel's error is to be found, to be sure, in his logic but also, in my view, in other parts of the logic [...]

[56] In the quick survey of the various Hegelian doctrines that I gave in the previous chapters, I have alluded in passing (because I was eager to move on to the problem of dialectics) to the relations of distincts [distinti], that is, speculative distinct concepts and not those of the naturalistic classifications. Now we must take a closer look because it is my firm belief that we can find the logical error there, with plenty of consequences, against which Hegel was unable to guard.

The philosophical concept, the concrete-universal or Idea, just as it is synthesis of opposites so it is synthesis of distinct concepts. For instance, we speak of the spirit or of spiritual activity in general, but we also speak at every instant of the particular forms of this spiritual activity. And while we consider all of them constitutive of a complete spirituality (whose deficiency offends us and compels us to find a remedy, while the partial or total absence frightens us as absurd or monstrous), we are then on guard and jealous so that one does not get confused with the other, and that is why we censure those who judge art with moral criteria, or morality with artistic criteria, or truth with utilitarian criteria, and so on. Because, if we were to forget to distinguish, one look at life would soon remind us that life shows us that even externally the spheres of activities are distinct – economic, scientific, moral, artistic, and the single man is now referred to as poet, now as industrialist, now as statesman, now as philosopher. Philosophy too would remind us because it does not express itself without being specified in aesthetics, logic, ethics, and so on. They are all philosophies, and yet each one is a philosophy distinct from the others.

These distinct concepts of which we have provided examples, and that are unity and distinction at the same time, form a relation or a rhythm that the theory of naturalistic or intellectualistic classification is unable to justify. Hegel understood this very well, which is why he never stopped fighting their schemes when, transferred in philosophy, the concepts were conceived as subordinates and co-ordinates, whereby a concept is placed as the foundation, then another is introduced, extraneous to the first one, and assumed to be the foundation of the division, almost as a knife with which we cut a focaccia (the first concept) into so many pieces that remain separate from one another. With this kind of procedure, with these results, there is no more unity of the universal. Reality breaks into so many elements that are extraneous and indifferent from one another; philosophy, as the thought of unity, is rendered impossible.

Hegel's abhorrence for this method of classification made him the first one to reject, even before Herbart (mistakenly celebrated as the first author to criticize it), the conception of the faculties of the soul, which Kant still followed. In an essay of 1802 he rejected that psychology as false because "it represents the spirit as a bag full of faculties" (Hegel, *Werke*, XVI, 130). In the *Encyclopedia*, as well as in other writings, he repeated again: "The feeling we have of the living unity of the spirit is opposed to being fragmented into different forces, whether faculty or activity, independently conceived from one another" (*Encyclopedia*, 379, see also 445). Note that Hegel, always *sollicitus servandi unitatem spiritus*, could have made this criticism with more right and consequence than could Herbart, who was incapable of reconciling his refutation of the faculties of the soul with his atomistic metaphysics, and with his ethics and aesthetics, which conformed to a catalogue of ideas, each separate from the other. But as it is usually the case, according to the opinion of writers of psychology manuals and histories of philosophy, Herbart was a revolutionary in matters of the spirit, while Hegel was believed to be almost a reactionary who preserved the classifications of scholasticism.

If distinct concepts cannot be posited separately and must be unified in their distinction, the logical theory of distinct concepts will be the theory not of classification but of implication. The concept will not be cut into pieces by an extraneous force but will be divided in itself by an internal movement, and in these self-distinctions it will be preserved as one. One distinct will be with respect to another distinct, not as something indifferent, but as an inferior degree is to a superior degree, and vice versa. The classification of reality must be substituted by the conception of degrees of the Spirit or, in general, of reality; the scheme of classifications must be replaced by the scheme of degrees.

Hegel's thinking started in this fashion, which was the only one conforming to the principle from which it moved: the concrete universal. His theory of degrees circulates in all of Hegel's writings, even though it is nowhere widely and expressly worked out. And even in this case it had precursors that we should analyse, and also in this case the philosopher to whom he is more akin is perhaps Giambattista Vico, who similarly differentiated by a series of degrees the spirit, languages, governments, laws, customs, and religions: the spirit as sense, imagination, and intellect; languages as divine mental language, heroic language, and articulated languages; governments as theocracies, aristocracies, and democracies; laws as of divine right, established by the gods, heroic or by force, and by human or fully unfolded human reason; and so on. Therefore, Vico too did not conceive philosophy as a pigeonhole of separate cells but as "an ideal eternal history on which the particular histories occur in time." But if Hegel did not know Vico's work, he had other stimuli for the solution he was seeking. There was the eighteenth century "sensism," and especially Condillac's doctrine, that seemed to him, notwithstanding the poverty of categories and their assumptions, to be worthwhile in so far as they included the attempt to make comprehensible the diversity of forms in the unity of the spirit, by showing their genesis. In reproaching Kant, who had simply enumerated the faculties and the categories by constructing tables, he added high praise for Fichte, who had declared the need for the "deduction" of categories. But he found the one and true precedent in Schelling's system of identity with its method of potentials [potenziare] whereby reality unfolds as a series of powers or of degrees: "The subject-object (this is how Schelling remembers his youthful conception, in his claim against Hegel), by virtue of its nature, objectifies itself, but from any objectification it returns victorious and shows itself every time at a higher power of subjectivity until, after having exhausted its every virtuality, it appears as the subject that triumphs over everything" (From Schelling's *Preface to Victor Cousin's Fragments*).

What does a theory of degrees entail? What are its terms, what is their relation? And what difference does it present to the theory of opposites with respect to the terms and relations? In the theory of degrees, any concept, and let this be concept _a_, is both distinct and united with concept _b_, which is superior to it in degree; thus if (to begin the exposition of the relation) _a_ is posited without _b_, _b_ cannot be posited without _a_. By taking the example of the relation of the concepts of art and philosophy, which I have analysed in my *Aesthetics*, or of poetry and prose, language and logic, intuition and thought, and so on, we can see that what appears to be at first an insoluble enigma and a riddle for empirical and classifying logic is resolved naturally in the speculative logic by means of the doctrine of degrees. It is not possible to place art and philosophy as two distinct and coordinated species of a gender to which they are both subordinate, and which is, for example, the cognitive form, in such a way that the presence of the first excludes the other, as it was the case with members of co-ordinates. There is a lot of evidence in the past and in the present of the many distinctions between poetry and prose – all very useless, all founded on arbitrary elements. But the problem is resolved once the relation is thought as distinction and unity at the same time: poetry can stay without prose (though it does not exclude it), but prose can never stay without poetry. Art does not exclude philosophy, but philosophy includes even art. In fact, philosophy does not exist in any other way than in words, images, metaphors, forms of languages – symbols that are its artistic side and so real and essential that where they are lacking, philosophy is also lacking, because an unexpressed philosophy is inconceivable: man thinks by speaking. The same demonstration is possible with the example of the other dyads of philosophical concepts: the shift from law to morality or the shift from perceptive conscience to legislative conscience. In this fashion, as Aristotle says, the real, which is one, is divided in itself, grows on itself, or, to say it with Vico, follows its ideal history, and in the last degree, which sums up in itself all previous ones, it reaches itself, entirely explicated or entirely unfolded.

If we pass now from the relation of degrees a and b (in our example, art and philosophy) to the synthesis of opposites, α, β, γ (in our example, being, not-being, and becoming), we can determine the differences between the two relations. A and b are two concepts of which the second is arbitrary and abstract without the first, but in its relation with the first is as real and concrete as the other. Instead, α and β outside γ are not two concepts but two abstractions. The only concrete concept is γ, becoming. If we apply the arithmetic symbols to the two relations, we have a dyad in the first one and a unity in the second one, or, if you wish, a triad, which is a triunity. If we wish to call dialectic (objective) both the synthesis of opposites and the relation of degrees, we must not forget that the dialectic has a different process from that of the other. If we wish to apply to the one relation and to the other Hegel's terminology of "moments" and "overcoming," which is at the same time a "suppressing" and a "preserving," we have to state that these denominations take on different meanings in each of these relations. In fact, in the theory of degrees the two moments, as I have indicated, are both concrete; in the synthesis of opposites they are both abstract: pure being and non-being. In the relation of degrees a is overcome by b, that is, it is suppressed as independent and preserved as dependent. The spirit, in passing from art to philosophy, denies art and preserves it, at the same time, as the expressive form of philosophy. In the relation of opposites, considered objectively, α and β, which are distinct from each other, are both suppressed and preserved, but only metaphorically because they never existed as the distinct concepts α and β.

These deep differences make it unacceptable to deal with each relation in the same way. Truth is not in the same relation to falsehood as it is to the good; the beautiful is not in the same relation to the ugly as it is to philosophical truth. Life without death and death without life are two false opposites whose truth is life, which is a relation of life and death, of itself and of its opposite. But truth without goodness and goodness without truth are not two falsehoods that are annulled in a third term. They are false conceptions that are resolved in a relation of degrees, in which truth and goodness are distinct and united at the same time. Goodness without truth is impossible, just as it is impossible to love without thinking. Truth without goodness is possible only in the sense that they coincide with the philosophical thesis of the priority of the theoretical spirit over the practical with the theorems of the autonomy of art and the autonomy of science [...]

[63] When we claim that the Spirit does not find satisfaction in art and, for this reason, is moved to find it in philosophy, we are correct, but one must not be led astray by metaphors. The Spirit that is no longer satisfied with artistic reflection is no longer artistic spirit, is already not in it; it is already incipient philosophical spirit. In the same way, the Spirit that is not satisfied with philosophical universality, action, and praxis, and thirsts for contemplation and dreams, is no longer philosophical spirit but is already aesthetic spirit, a determinate aesthetic spirit that begins to fall in love with some vision and intuition. Just as in the latter case and in the former, the antithesis does not occur within the degree [already] overcome. Just as philosophy is not contradicted by philosophy, so art is not contradicted by art, and everyone knows the great satisfaction, the deep and undisturbed delight, that we take in works of art. The individual Spirit passes from art to philosophy, and back again from philosophy to art, in the same way that it goes from one form of art to another or from one problem of philosophy to another: that is, not because of inherent contradictions in any of these forms in their distinction, but because of the inherent contradictions in the real, which is becoming. The universal spirit goes from a to b, and from b to a, not for any other necessity than its eternal nature, which is to be both art and philosophy, theory and praxis, or whatever else is being determined. This is so true that if this ideal passing were to be moved from the contradictions inherent in a given degree, it would not be possible to return to that degree that was recognized to be contradictory. To return would imply a degeneration or a regress. And who would dare consider aesthetic contemplation arising from philosophy to be a degeneration or a regress? Who could judge erroneous and contradictory one or the other of the essential forms of the human spirit? The passing of ideal history

is not a passing or, better, is an eternal passing that, from the point of view of eternity, is Being.

Hegel never made the very important distinction between the theory of opposites and the theory of distincts, as I have tried to do. He conceived the relation of degrees dialectically as a dialectics of opposites and applied to this relation the triadic form, which is proper to the synthesis of opposites. The theory of distinct concepts and the theory of opposites became for him all one thing. It was almost inevitable that this would happen because of that special psychological condition of those who discover a new aspect of the real (in this case, the synthesis of opposites), who become tyrannized by this discovery, inebriated by the new wine of that truth, and see it everywhere in front of them, and are led to conceive everything according to the new formula. It was almost inevitable that it should happen like this, also because of the close and fine relations that bind the theory of distinct concepts to the theory of opposites, and both to the theory of the concrete universal or the idea. In the theory of degrees there are also, as in the theory of opposites, various moments to be overcome, that is, to be suppressed and preserved at the same time. Even in the theory of degrees there is unity and distinction, as in the theory of opposites. To detect the differences was reserved for another historical period, when the new wine was seasoned and rested.

We can find proof in every passage of Hegel's writings of this failed distinction or of this confusion where the relation of distincts is always presented as a relation of thesis and synthesis. Thus, in anthropology we have thesis, natural soul; antithesis, sensitive soul; synthesis, real soul. In psychology: thesis, theoretical spirit; antithesis, practical spirit; synthesis, free spirit. Or, thesis, intuition; antithesis, representation; synthesis, thought. In the *Philosophy of Practice*: thesis, law; antithesis, morality; synthesis, ethics. Or still, thesis, family; antithesis, civil society; synthesis, state. In the sphere of the Absolute Spirit: thesis, art; antithesis, religion; synthesis, philosophy. Or in Subjective Logic: thesis, concept; antithesis, judgment; synthesis, syllogism. In the Logic of the Idea: thesis, life; antithesis, knowledge; synthesis, absolute idea. And so on. This is the first instance of that abuse of the triadic form that offends those who approach Hegel's system, and it is rightly seen as abuse. In fact, how can one accept that religion is the non-being of art, and that art and religion are two abstractions whose truth is only in philosophy, a synthesis of both? Or that the practical Spirit is the negation of the theoretical, and that representation is the negation of intuition, and that civil society is the negation of the family and of the morality of law? And that all these concepts are unthinkable outside their syntheses – free spirit, thought, state, ethics – in the same way as being and non-being that are only true in becoming? To be sure, Hegel was not always faithful to the triadic form (already in some of his youthful writings he stated that *"quadratum est lex naturae, triangulum mentis"*). And more often, in certain developments, he mitigated the errors of the triadic form, but there is no particular determination that can suppress the division that has been assumed as foundation. At other times, the triadic form seems almost an imaginary way to express thoughts that do not arrive at their substantial truth, but to accept this kind of interpretation would be the same as discrediting that form in its logical value, that is, in the value that it must preserve fully in the dialectic or in the synthesis of opposites. On the other hand, to defend Hegel's statements with extrinsic arguments would be to proceed as a lawyer who wants to win by being clever and not with the truth, or as a barrator who places the gold coins upfront so that in the confusion he can slip in the false ones.

The error is not such that it can be corrected as we go, nor is it an error of expression [dicitura]. It is a substantial error that even though it may appear insignificant from the summary that I have provided, as an exchange between theory of distincts and theory of opposites, it has very serious consequences because on it, if I am correct, depends everything that is wrong with Hegel's system.

The Internal Structure of the *New Science*

(The Philosophy of G.B. Vico, chap. 3, pp. 37–44)

[37] The scarce clarity concerning the relation between philosophy and philology, and the lack of distinction between the two different manners of conceiving the reduction of philology to science, are the reasons and the consequences of the obscurity that looms over the *New Science*. With this name we understand it to include all the system of research and doctrines that Vico produced between 1720 and 1730, in fact until 1744, and that he elaborated mainly in three works: *De uno universi iuris principio et fine uno,* and in the first and second *New Science,* which finds in the definitive edition of 1744 its most developed and mature form, to which one mainly refers.

The *New Science,* according to the various meanings of the terms and relations between philosophy and philology, amounts to three orders of research – philosophical, historical, and empirical – and contains altogether a philosophy of mind, a history or group of histories, and a social science. To the first category, philosophy, belong ideas, expressed in some axioms, or *degnità*, and spread out in the entire work: on the imagination, on fantastic universals, on the intellect and on logical universals, on myth, on religion, on moral judgment, on power and the law, on what is certain and on what is true, on passion, on providence, and on all other determinations regarding the course or the necessary development of the mind or the human spirit.

To the second category, history, belongs a sketch of the universal history of primitive races after the Flood and the origins of various civilizations: the character of barbaric or ancient heroic societies from Greece, and especially Rome, under the aspects of religion, law, language, and political constitution; the inquiry on primitive poetry, which is expanded to determine the genesis and the character of Homeric poems; the history of the struggle between patricians and plebeians; and the origins of democracy, which focuses primarily on Rome. The return of barbarism, that is, the Middle Ages, is also studied under all aspects of life and contrasted with primitive barbaric societies. Finally, in the category of empirical sciences, there is an attempt to establish a uniform course of nations regarding the sequence of both political forms and other theoretical and practical manifestations of life and of the many types that Vico outlines: patricians and plebeians; feudalism; parental authority and the family; symbolic law; metaphorical language; hieroglyphics; and so on.

Now if these three orders of research and doctrines had been logically distinct in Vico's mind and only literarily mixed up and included in the same work, it could have been disorderly, disproportionate, and discordant to the reader but not really obscure. For, after all, it cannot be said, really, that the *New Science* – at least the second one, namely, the definitive version that Vico gave of his thought – lacked in general design, since it was well conceived. The work is divided into five books. The first should have contained the general principles, that is, its philosophy. The second, besides a brief allusion to ancient universal history, should have described the life of barbaric societies and served as an appendix to the third book, on the discovery of the true Homer, that is, on the conspicuous aspect of barbaric poetry. The fourth should have outlined the empirical science of the course taken by all nations, and the fifth should have exemplified the *ricorso* with the specific case of the Middle Ages. Yet despite this fine architecture, the second

New Science is the most accomplished, but also the most obscure, of Vico's works.

Even if Vico, who had very clear ideas on what he wanted to do, had employed an unusual terminology or a very concise form of exposition, full of allusions and unexpressed assumptions, he would have been without a doubt a difficult writer, but he would not have been obscure. However, this hypothesis does not correspond to reality, because Vico makes very little use of scholastic terms and favours popular and common expressions. He is a solid writer but not a laconic writer, and he likes to repeat his ideas and to repeat them often and with great insistence. He puts everything on the table, all the erudite material that suggested his ideas. Finally, it cannot be said that Vico lacked a full conscience of his discoveries, because this conscience is more or less lacking in all thinkers and no one can have full conscience of all of them. The real obscurity that one remarks in Vico's works, and that at times even he observed without ever finding the cause, is not superficial and is not produced by external or accidental causes but consists, truly, in an obscurity of ideas, in a lack of understanding of certain connections, and in their substitution with erroneous connections, and in the arbitrary element that introduces itself in thought or, to state it simply, in truly real errors. One could rewrite the *New Science* by reordering it, changing or clearing up the terminology. (I myself have tried this test, but the obscurity persists; in fact, it increases because through this translation the work, in losing the original form, loses that murky but powerful effectiveness that sometimes can take the place of clarity, which, where it does not shed light, stirs the spirit of the reader and spreads the waves of thinking almost by sympathetic vibrations.)

The reason for the obscurity of Vico's error or errors is the lack of distinction or the confusion that we have already noted in his epistemology with the relation between philosophy, history, and empirical science and consists of his actual thinking about the problems of the spirit and of human history, which result from observing how philosophy, history, and empirical science are converted time after time into one another, and by damaging one another they produce those perplexities, ambiguities, exaggerations, and temerities that tend to disturb the reader of the *New Science*. The philosophy of mind now poses as empirical science, now as history; the empirical science now poses as philosophy, now as history; and historical propositions now acquire the universality of philosophical principles, now the generality of empirical schemes. For instance, the philosophy of humanity takes on the task

of determining the forms, categories, or ideal moments of the spirit
in their necessary succession, and for this reason it well deserves the
name or the definition of ideal eternal history on which particular histories unfold in time, since it is impossible to conceive any fragment of
real history, insignificant as it may be, where that ideal history is not at
work.

But, because, for Vico, ideal history is also the empirical determination of the order in which the forms of civilization, states, languages,
styles, and poetry succeed one another, it happens that he conceives
the empirical series to be identical to the ideal series, and possessing
all its virtues, hence axiom #348 that its ideal history should always
be verified with facts: "even if in eternity infinite worlds were to be
born from time to time." This is openly false because there is no reason
that the empirical aristocracies of Greece or Rome should be repeated
forever (as it is claimed that "they had to, must, and will have to") and
that civilizations should rise or fall precisely in the way that ancient
ones rose and fell. And while this empirical course is being absolutized,
the ideal course becomes veiled with an empirical shadow because,
once it is made identical to the other, it receives the empirical character
of the other, and, though being eternal and extra-temporal initially, it
becomes temporal.

The same can be said of the single forms of the spirit, which, being
ideal and extra-temporal, are always in every single fact, but since Vico
confuses them with real and concrete facts, which empirical science
establishes in its schemes, soon after he has proposed them, he obscures
their ideal form and distinction. It is true that the moment of power
is not the power of justice but the empirical type of barbaric society
based on force, precisely because it is a representative and approximate
determination and refers to a concrete and total state of things; it contains not just force but also justice. And when that ideal moment and
that type are exchanged one with the other and are taken to be identical, the philosophical concept of force, on the one hand, becomes confused with that of justice and, in becoming hybrid, contradictory, and
incoherent, becomes deformed; on the other hand, the empirical type
of barbaric society is exaggerated and hardened. The confusion of the
philosophical element with the empirical is exemplified by axiom #14
that defines the nature of things – "The nature of things is nothing else
but its origin at a given time and in a given form; as long as it is such,
it originates this way and in no other way" – in which form and time,
the ideal and the empirical genesis, are paired. Similarly, while it is very

true that history has to proceed in accordance with philosophy and that what is philosophically repugnant cannot have ever historically occurred, because for Vico philosophy is not distinct from empirical science, in instances where he lacks the documentation and therefore no philosophy is applicable he feels nonetheless certain of the truth, and, in filling the void with a conjecture that the scheme of empirical science provides to him, he is deceived in thinking that he has made use of "metaphysical proof."

Or when he finds himself before some doubtful fact, instead of waiting for the discovery of other documentation to clear it up, he resolves it by taking it, as he says, "in conformity to the law," that is, to the empirical scheme that is certainly legitimate as a hypothesis. But that hypothesis for Vico is a "truth mediated in idea," so that checking the facts, which he also recommends for confirmation, should be superfluous; or if the facts should turn out to be contrary, at fault are the facts or the appearance but never the hypothesis, which is asserted as a certain truth because it is philosophical. Hence Vico's tendency, as they say, to do violence to facts.

These examples ought to suffice to point to the deep-seated structural flaws of the *New Science* and to establish one of the tenets of our analysis and of our critique of Vico's philosophy, during which we will suggest many more examples and we will clarify better those we have already given. But the other tenet that we must establish is that the flaw is the flaw of an extremely robust organism and that the type of research that Vico confused is the result of actual research of extraordinary novelty, truth, and importance. In short, it is the flaw that we frequently come across in very original and creative minds who rarely perfect their discoveries in all their particular details, whereas those minds that are less creative tend to be more exact and consistent. Depth and insight do not always go together and with the same intensity, and Vico, though he was not very acute, had always depth.

Light and darkness, truth and error, alternate and intersect almost at every turn of the *New Science* and are differently understood according to the different approaches of readers and critics. In fact, in Vico's case these differences can be noticed even more clearly. There are those who are reluctant and suspicious, ready to remark on every little contradiction, who are relentless in demanding proof for every statement, determined to employ the pincers of dilemma that crush without mercy a poor great man. For them, Vico's work (and many others of the same quality) is a closed book that, at best, can offer them the excuse for one more so-called demolition, which they perform with great ease and pleasure, though with little success because when the man they have killed is dead, he is even more alive than before.

But there are others who, when the first word goes straight to their heart and the first light of truth flashes in their eyes, are full of desire and let themselves go with confidence. They are intoxicated with enthusiasm, they overlook defects, they are not aware of difficulties, or, if they are, they iron out the difficulties right away and justify the flaws in the simplest way, and when, by chance, they write, their writings tend to be "apologies." For them, sorry to say, the *New Science* is too much of an open book. To be sure, if between these two opposite tendencies there were not a third one, if we had to decide between either of the two, it would be preferable to sin for too much love than for cold indifference. At least, too much faith allows for some inkling of truth, whereas no faith at all allows for none. But a third way is possible, and it is the duty of the critic not to lose sight of the light, while not forgetting the darkness; to reach the spirit by going beyond the letter, but also not to neglect the letter – on the contrary, to return to it time after time, managing to remain a free interpreter but not an inventive one, to be a passionate lover but not blind.

The two established tenets, the flaws and virtues that have been recognized proper to Vico's mind, and his brilliant confusion or his confusing brilliance require, therefore, as a general hermeneutical canon the separation, through analysis, of pure philosophy from the empiricism and history with which it is mingled and almost integrated (and vice versa), and the observation, each time, of the effects and the causes of the combination. The dross cannot be ignored, because it is mixed with the gold in its pure state of nature, but it must not prevent us from recognizing and purifying the gold; literally speaking, history must be history, without doubt, but it is not history unless it is intelligent.

History

The selections on history are similar to those in Croce's *Anthology*. The first selection, "History and Chronicle," from *Teoria e storia della storiografia* (*History: Its Theory and Practice*), discusses the important issue of the difference between history and chronicle, with respect to the notion of history as contemporary history. History is contemporary not in the ordinary sense of the word but in the sense of the unity of history and life, and thought and life, which is intrinsic to every history. However, when the link between history and life is broken, all that is left is dead history, and this is what the chronicle is, an accumulation of empty words: "Mere narrative, therefore, is but an empty combination of empty words or formulas asserted by an act of will." True history is an act of thought; the chronicle is an act of will. "History is living history; chronicle is dead history. History is contemporary history; chronicle is past history."

The second selection, from *La storia come pensiero e come azione* (*History as the Story of Liberty*), brings up the importance of the identity of philosophy and history. Philosophy by itself is metaphysics; only philosophy that is history, at the same time, is true philosophy. The "philosophy of history," which Hegel promotes, is neither history nor philosophy. It is the result of a mental effort, of a lack, of an *"inopia"* of the mind, similar to myth. It is allegory, not philosophy. The philosophy that took its place is philosophy *as* history: "What took its place is no longer philosophy but history or, which is the same, philosophy as history, and history as philosophy: philosophy-history, whose principle is the identity of the universal and the individual, of intellect and intuition, and declares as arbitrary or illegitimate any separation of the two elements, which in reality are only one."

The third selection, from *Il carattere della filosofia moderna* (The character of modern philosophy), deals with Croce's notion of philosophy as absolute historicism. This is a reworking of Hegel's definition of philosophy as absolute Spirit or Idea, which for Croce is didactic and metaphysical, or allegorical. Once philosophy is reformulated in terms of the identity of philosophy and history, there cannot be any metaphysical misunderstanding or didacticism, or allegory; absolute idealism becomes absolute historicism. This possibility, however, as I have indicated in the "Philosophy" chapter, is predicated on how we read a philosophical statement that may appear to be metaphysics to the non-philosopher: just empty and meaningless words: "Outside of this serious historical interpretation even the theories of philosophers take on, similarly to metaphysical systems, the aspect of a series of empty assertions that are in conflict with one another, as they appear in fact to the uninitiated, those who do not think by rethinking them" (CFM, 27). A true philosopher, as Croce demonstrates in his critiques of Hegel and of Vico (but also of other philosophers), rethinks the statements of philosophy and reformulates them in his own words. This is what Croce does in the particular instance when Hegel's didactic or allegorical philosophy of spirit or absolute spirit is reformulated as "absolute historicism": "The reduction of didactic philosophy to a 'methodology of historiography' (according to the definition that I proposed many years ago) closes the way to a possible metaphysical misunderstanding of the philosophy of spirit and of absolute spirit and confers to it the more fitting name of 'absolute historicism" (CFM, 28). Only the sceptics doubt the resurgence of didactic philosophy as a philosophy of absolute historicism, or the identity of philosophy and history. One must ignore their inane laughter at a philosophy in ruins.

The separate section on *La storia dell'età barocca in Italia (The History of the Baroque Age in Italy)* is an example of "negative" history and deals with a historical period, the seventeenth century, about which Croce would have preferred not to write; just as he would have preferred not to write about Futurism, which nonetheless, "somehow," also finds its way into this history of the Baroque. See the commentary at the beginning of the "Baroque" section.

"Storia e cronaca"
(Teoria e storia della storiografia, pp. 13–29)

[13] We usually define contemporary history as the history of a segment in time that we consider to be a very near past: the last fifty years,

or ten years or a year or a month or a day and, may be, the last hour or the last minute. But, strictly speaking, by "contemporary" we ought to mean only that history that originates immediately, as the action is being completed, as the conscience of that act: for instance, the history that I myself make as I start composing these pages and which is the thought of my composition, joined necessarily to the work of composition. The term "contemporary" would be correct in this case precisely because, like any spiritual act, it is outside time (a before and after) and is formed "at the same time" as the act to which it is joined and from which it is distinguished not chronologically but ideally. Instead, "non-contemporary history," "past history," is the one that already finds a formed history before and originates therefore as a critique of that history, whether it is a million years old or just an hour.

However, if we consider more closely this history that has already taken place, which we call or is called "non-contemporary history" or "past history," if it is really history, that is, if it has meaning and is not just empty discourse, it is contemporary and does not differ at all from the other. As for the other, its condition is that the fact of the story that it narrates vibrates in the soul of the historian or, to use his terminology, that we have intelligible documents before us. And if several stories of the fact are united or mixed, it matters only if that fact is being presented in a more interesting way, but not that it has lost its present effectiveness. What used to be stories or judgments are now also facts, also "documents" to be interpreted and judged. History is constructed never on narratives but always on documents, or on narratives reduced to documents and treated as such. And if contemporary history stems directly from life, so does what we usually call non-contemporary history because it is evident that only an interest in present life can move us to investigate a fact of the past that, in so far as it unites with an interest in present life, does not respond to a past interest but to a present one. This has been said and repeated many times in many ways in the empirical formulas of the historians and constitutes, if not its deep meaning, the reason of the somewhat trite saying that "history is the teacher of life" (*magistra vitae*).

I have recalled these formulas of historical techniques to eliminate the paradoxical aspect of the proposition that "any true history is contemporary history." The correctness of this proposition is easily confirmed, and amply and abundantly exemplified, by the reality of historiography as long as one does not fall into the error of taking haphazardly all the works of historians or of a group of them, and by the reference to an abstract being, or to ourselves, to ask what present interest leads us to write or read those stories. What is our present interest in the Peloponnesian or Mithridatic wars, the events of Mexican art or of Arabic philosophy? For me, at this moment there is none, and therefore, for me, at this moment those stories are not histories. If anything, they are simply titles of history books and have been or will be stories for those who thought them or will think about them, and they will be for me, when I think or will think about them, when I elaborate them according to my spiritual needs.

If, however, we adhere to real history, to the history that we are really thinking, at the moment that we think of it, it will be easy to notice that it is perfectly identical to the most personal and contemporary stories. When the unfolding of the culture of my historical moment (and it is superfluous and probably not even exact to add, of me as an individual) opens before me the problem of Hellenic civilization, of Platonic philosophy, or of a particular aspect of Attic custom, that problem is as bound to my being as is the history of a business deal that I am conducting, of a love affair that I am having, or of a danger that is threatening me. And I investigate it with the same concern, I am torn by the same sense of unhappiness, until I am able to resolve it. In that case, Hellenic life is present within me and presses me and attracts me or torments me, just as does the face of my rival, of the woman I love, of my favourite son for whom I am anxious. And so it happens, or it has happened, or it will happen of the Mithridatic wars, of Mexican art, and of all the other things that I mentioned before as examples.

Once we accept that "contemporary" is not a characteristic of a type of history (as is claimed with good reasons in empirical classifications) but an intrinsic trait of every history, we have to conceive the relation of history to life as one of unity, not in the sense of an abstract identity but in the sense of a synthetic unity that entails both the distinction and the unity of terms. Since to speak of a history of which we do not possess the documents seems to be just as extravagant as speaking of the existence of anything of which we claim, at the same time we lack one of its essential conditions of existence. A history without any relation to documents would be an unverifiable story, and because the reality of history is in its verifiability, and the narrative in which it is concretized is a historical narrative only in so far as it is the critical exposition of a document (intuition and reflection, awareness and self-awareness, et cetera), a story of that kind, devoid of meaning and truth, would not exist as history. How could a history of painting be written by someone who was planning to give a critical account but had not seen the works and enjoyed them? Or how intelligible would it be for someone who did not have the artistic experience presumed by the author? How could one compose a history of philosophy without the works of philosophers, or at least their fragments? How could one write a history of a feeling or of custom, for instance, of Christian humility or chivalry, without the ability to relive or, better, relive effectively these particular spiritual conditions?

On the other hand, once the indissoluble bond between life and thought has been asserted in history, the doubts that arose on the certainty and utility of history suddenly and totally disappear to the point that one can no longer even conceive them. How could we doubt what is a present product of our spirit? How could knowledge that resolves a problem borne from the bosom of life be useless?

II

But can the link between document and narrative, life and history, ever be broken? The answer is already implied in what was said about the histories whose documents have been lost or, to state a more general and fundamental case, when the documents are no longer alive in the spirit. In what was said, the acknowledgment was also implicit that each one of us finds himself in this condition time after time, with respect to this or that part of history. The history of Hellenic painting is for us, generally, to a large extent, a history without documents. Histories without documents are all those we read about people and do not know exactly where they lived, the thoughts and feelings that moved them, the individual physiognomy of the works they made. Or the literary and philosophical works of which we do not have the texts, or, having them and even reading them, we are unable to penetrate their intimate spirit because of a lack of background knowledge, because of an obstinate unwillingness of our disposition, or because of a momentary distraction.

In all these cases, once the link has been broken, what remains is no longer history (because history was nothing more than that link), though we can still continue to call it history just as we still call the corpse of a man "man." This does not mean that what is left is nothing (not even the corpse is properly nothing). If it were nothing, we might as well say that the link is indissoluble because the nothing is never real. And if it is nothing, if it is something, what is the narrative without the document? A history of Hellenic painting, according to the stories that have come down to us or that have been invented by modern scholars, when we look closely, comes down to a series of names of painters – Apollodorus, Polignotus of Thasos, Zeuxis, Apelles, et cetera – with the addition of biographical anecdotes; to a series of titles of paintings – the Destruction of Troy, the Fight of the Amazons, the Battle of Marathon, Helen, Achilles, Slander, et cetera – some of them accompanied by some detailed description; to a series of blames or praises to various degrees – names, anecdotes, subjects, judgments – ordered somewhat chronologically. But the names of painters without a direct knowledge of their works are empty names, and empty are the anecdotes, and empty are the descriptions of the subjects, and empty are the judgments of approval or disapproval, and empty is the chronological order, because they are just numbers that do not add up to a real development, of which no thought can be realized in us because we lack the constitutive elements. If those verbal formulas tell us anything, we owe it to the little we know of ancient painting from fragments, or from secondary works, from copies or analogous works of art and poetry. But beside that, the history of Hellenic painting is just a context of empty words.

Or, if you prefer, words "empty of determined meaning," because we are not denying that by mentioning the name of a painter we think of a painter, and maybe an Athenian painter, and that by mentioning the name "battle" or "Helen" we think of a battle or a fight among hoplites, or a beautiful woman, maybe similar to those with which we are familiar in Hellenic plastic representations. But we think indifferently of one or the other of the numberless facts recalled by those names, and that is why their content is indeterminate, and this indeterminateness of content is their emptiness.

As in this example, all the stories detached from their living documents are empty narratives, and, because they are empty, they are also deprived of truth. Is it true or not true that there was a painter called Polygnotus who painted the portrait of Miltiades in the Pecile? Someone will say that it is true because someone or many who knew him saw the work and they attest to its existence. Instead, we ought to say that it was true for those witnesses, but, for us, it is neither true nor false, or, which is the same, it is true only on the authority of those witnesses, that is, for extrinsic reasons – whereas truth always requires intrinsic reasons. And just as the proposition is not true (neither true nor false), it is not even useful, because where there is nothing, the king loses his rights, and where the elements of a problem are lacking, the possibility, the actual will and the actual need to resolve it, is also lacking. So that to narrate those empty details is useless to the actuality of our life. Life is a present, and the history that has become an empty narrative is a past, an irrevocable if not an absolute past, certainly, in the present moment.

Only empty words are left, and empty words are sounds or the graphic sounds that represent them, and they stay together or keep together not because of an act of thought that thinks them (in which case they would be quickly filled) but because of an act of will that believes it to be advantageous to keep those words empty or half empty. Mere narrative, therefore, is only an empty combination of empty words or formulas asserted by an act of will.

By this definition we have arrived at the true distinction between history and chronicle that we have been looking for. We looked for it in vain because we wanted to find it in the different quality of the facts that each took as its object. For instance, we attributed to the chronicle the remembrance of individual facts, and to history general facts, to the former private facts, to the latter public ones, as if the general were not always individual, and the individual general, the public not always private, and the private public. To history we attributed the memory of important facts (that is, memoranda), and to the chronicle less important ones, as if the importance of a fact was not relative to the situation in which we found ourselves, so that for a man bothered by a mosquito the evolution of this minuscule insect would not be less important than Xerxes's expedition! To be sure, even in these erroneous distinctions we observe a correct attitude, which is to establish a difference between history and chronicle in the notion of what is interesting or not interesting (the general, not the particular, is interesting; big, not small, is interesting, et cetera). A correct attitude can also be observed in other respects that are usually brought to bear, like the solid bond that exists in history, and the disconnectedness, instead, of the chronicle; the logical order of the former, and the purely chronological order of the latter; how the first delves deeply into events, while the latter remains on the surface or on the outside; and so on. But the differential character in these cases is rather more metaphorical than thought out, and with metaphors, when they are not employed as simple expressions of thought, one loses a moment later what one had gained a moment earlier. In truth, chronicle and history cannot be distinguished as two forms of history that occur at the same time or in which one is subordinate to the other, but they are two different spiritual modes. History is living history; chronicle is dead history. History is contemporary history; chronicle is past history. History is primarily an act of thought; chronicle, an act of will. Any history becomes chronicle when it is no longer thought but only remembered in abstract words, words that at one time were concrete and expressive. Chronicle is even the history of philosophy written by those who do not know philosophy or who do not read it; instead, what we would think of as chronicle is actually history. It is what the Montecassino monk wrote – "1001. Beatus Dominus migravit ad Christum. 1002. Hoc anno venerunt Saraceni super Capuam. 1004. Terremotus ingens hunc montem exagitsavit, etc." – the monk who remembered these facts and lamented the departure of Saint Domenic, who was terrified by the human and natural calamities that afflicted his land, and saw in the unfolding of these events the outstretched hand of God. This does not exclude the possibility that the same monk may have thought of this history as a chronicle when he transcribed the cold formulas without representing or thinking about a content, but with the only aim in mind of transcribing these memories for the sole purpose of handing them down to those who would live in Montecassino after him.

But finding the true distinction between history and chronicle, which is a formal distinction (that is, really real), not only frees us from the tiring and sterile search for material distinctions (that is, fantastic), but it also enables us to reject a very common preconception, that of the priority of the chronicle over history: "Primo Annales (chronicles) fuer, post Historiae factae sunt," according to the saying by the ancient grammarian Marius Victorinus, which has been repeated, generalized, and universalized. But an analysis of the genesis and character of the two systems and attitudes demonstrates precisely the opposite: first History and then Chronicle, first the living and then the dead. To originate history from the chronicle would be like extracting life from a corpse, which is the residue of life, as the chronicle is the residue of history.

III

History detached from the living document and made chronicle is no longer a spiritual act but a thing, a complex of sounds or other signs. But the document detached from life is also nothing but a thing, similar to the other, the sum total of sounds and other signs: for instance, the sounds and letters through which a law is communicated; the lines inscribed in marble that exemplify a religious feeling by means of the figure of a god; and a pile of bones that at one time constituted the body of a man or an animal.

Do empty narratives and dead documents really exist? In a way they do not, because external things do not exist outside the spirit, and we already know that the chronicle as empty narrative exists because the spirit produces it and keeps it by an act of will (it may be appropriate to remark once again that such an act brings with it a new act of conscience and thought), by an act of will that abstracts the sound from the thought in which sound had its certainty and concreteness. Similarly, those dead documents exist in so far as they are manifestations of a new life, just as the lifeless body is also, after all, part of the process of vital creation, although it may appear in decomposition and as something dead with respect to a particular form of life. But just as empty sounds, which already enclose the thought of a history, are still called "narratives" in memory of the thought, so those manifestations of a new life are still considered traces of the life that preceded them, but are in fact spent.

And now, after all these deductions we can understand the distinction that is often made by modern theorists of historical sources between narratives and documents or, as the formula goes, between traditions and residues or remains (*Überbleibsel*, *Überreste*). A distinction that is irrational at the empirical level and can be taken as a typical example of the inappropriate introduction of speculative thought in empiricism. It is so irrational that one clashes right away against the difficulty of not being able to distinguish what one wanted to distinguish. And an empty "narrative," considered as a thing, adjusts to any other thing that one can call a "document." On the other hand, in keeping with the distinction, one comes across the further difficulty of having to construct history on the basis of two different types of data (by keeping one foot on the shore and the other in the river), that is to say, by making use of two parallel instances, where one refers constantly to the other. And when one tries to determine the relation between the two types of sources to avoid the uncomfortable parallelism, it happens that either one is said to be superior to the other and the distinction disappears, because the superior form is resolved and annuls the inferior one, or a third term is postulated in which the two forms are united by being differentiated, and this is another way to declare them inexistent in that abstraction. Therefore, it does not seem to me insignificant that the division between stories and documents has not found favour among empirical theorists who are not embarrassed by such subtleties and are happy to group historical sources with written and pictorial sources, or in other similar ways.

In Germany it was championed by Gustav Droysen (who was strongly disposed towards philosophy) in his famed *Outline of the Principles of History*, a work that has become successful with other theoreticians who, because of the wealth of philosophical tradition in that country, are hybrid empiricists – "systematic" or "pedantic," as they are judged in Latin countries. There is pedantry, to be sure, in that inappropriate philosophy, which, however, is healthy because of the contradictions that it accumulates and that wake up the minds from their empirical slumber and make them see that, where there are supposed to be things, there are instead spiritual acts; where, by contrast, they saw the terms of an incompatible dualism, there was in fact relation and unity! The division of sources into narratives and documents, and the superiority given to documents over narratives, and the asserted necessity of narratives as subordinate but necessary elements, posit almost a mythology or an allegory that represents in historical thinking, in a fantastic way, the relation of life and thought, of document and criticism.

Document and criticism, life and thought, are the true sources of history, the two elements of historical synthesis, and as such they are not before history, that is, before the synthesis – in the way that we imagine fountains to be before water is drawn from them by those with a pail – but within history itself, within the synthesis that constitutes it and by which it is constituted. Hence the idea of a history that has its sources outside itself is another notion that needs to be demystified, together with that of a history that has the chronicle as its antecedent: two erroneous mystifications that, in the end, converge into one. Sources as things, in the extrinsic sense of the empiricists, are similar to chronicles, which are a class of these things, not prior but after history. History would have a hard time being born from something that comes after it, or if it expected to be born from external things! Things are born of things, not of thoughts. A history that came from things would be a thing, namely, the inexistent to which we have alluded before.

Still, if it seems that the chronicle and the documents come before history and its extrinsic sources, there must be a reason. The human spirit retains the mortal spoils of history, the empty narratives, the chronicles. The same spirit gathers the traces of past life, the residues, the documents and tries to keep them unchanged as much as possible or to restore them when they have been altered. What is the purpose of these acts of will that are carried out to maintain the empty and the dead? Perhaps the illusion and the foolishness that make mortal man, when he is dead, linger at the margins of Dis, erecting houses of the dead, sepulchres. But sepulchres are neither illusions nor foolishness, rather moral acts with which we assert, symbolically, the immortality of the work accomplished by the individuals who, even though dead, are alive in our memory and in those who come after. It is an act of life, useful to life; it transcribes empty stories and gathers dead documents. The moment will come when they will make it possible for us to reproduce in our enriched spirit our past history, making it present.

For this reason, dead history lives again, and past history becomes present, as the unfolding of life requires. Greeks and Romans laid in their sepulchres until the European spirit came of age and reawakened them. Primitive forms, crude and barbaric, were forgotten, little understood or misunderstood, until that new phase of the European spirit, which took the name of Romanticism or Restoration, did not "sympathize" with them, that is, did not recognize them as being its own present interest. So much history that for us is chronicle, so many documents that for us are now silent will speak again from time to time when they are struck by the spark of life.

These revivals have entirely internal motivations, and there is no document, copy or narrative that can actualize them; in fact, they themselves gather in copies and bring before them the documents and the narratives that without them would remain spread out and stagnant. It is impossible to understand anything of the actual historical process if we do not begin from the principle that the Spirit itself is history and the maker of history at every moment, and the result of previous history. The Spirit carries within itself the entire history that coincides then with itself. To forget an aspect of history and to remember another is but the very rhythm of the life of the spirit that works by being determined and by individualizing itself; and it always determines and individualizes the previous determinations and individualizations in order to create even richer ones. The spirit would relive its history, so to speak, even without those external things that are called narratives and documents, but these external things are elements that it fashions and are preliminary acts that it accomplishes in order to actualize that vital internal conjuring in whose process they are resolved. This is how the spirit asserts and keeps jealously the "memories of the past."

What each one of us does at every instant, by writing in our diaries the dates and events relative to our work (chronicle), or by filling drawers with ribbons or dried flowers (allow me to offer this sublime image as an example of collecting documents), is exemplified, on a larger scale, almost by delegation of the entire society, by a class of workers called philologists and, specifically, scholars when they collect testimonies and narratives, and archivists and archaeologists when they collect documents and monuments, just as the places in which they keep these objects (the "white and silent houses of the dead") are called libraries, archives, museums. Can we blame the scholars, archivists, and archaeologists who fulfil a necessary service and are therefore useful and important? Nonetheless, we are in the habit of making fun of them and looking at them with pity. It is true that sometimes they ask for this reaction because of their naive claims to being the custodians of history and, at their will, unlocking its sources, from which parched society can attain them – that history which, instead, is in all of us and whose source is in our breast. Only our breast is the crucible in which the certain is converted into the true, and philology, uniting with philosophy, produces history.

Historical Knowledge as All Knowledge

(*La storia come pensiero e come azione*, chap. 5, pp. 26–30)

[26] It is not enough to say that history is historical judgment; one has to add that every judgment is historical judgment or, in short, history. If judgment is the relation of subject and predicate, the subject, namely, the fact that one is judging, whatever it may be, is always a historical fact, a becoming, an ongoing process because stationary facts do not exist, nor are they conceivable in the world of reality. Even the most obvious judging perception is historical judgment (if it did not judge, it would not even be perception, but blind and mute sensation). For example, the judgment that the object I see in front of my foot is a stone, and that it will not fly away by itself like a bird at the sound of my steps, necessitates that I push it with my foot or my cane, because the stone is really an ongoing process that resists the forces of disintegration or gives in a little at a time, so my judgment refers to an aspect of its history. However, we cannot stop here, but we must draw a further consequence, namely, that historical judgment is not just any order of knowledge but knowledge itself, the form that fills everything and exhausts the cognitive field, leaving no room for anything else.

In reality, any concrete knowing can only be at par with historical judgment, tied to life, namely, to action, a moment of its suspension or of its expectation, aimed at removing, as we said, the obstacle that it encounters when it does not discern clearly the situation from which it will have to burst out in its determinateness and distinctiveness.

A knowing for a knowing, differently from what some may imagine, not only has nothing of the aristocratic or of the sublime, modelled as it is, actually, on the idiotic pastime of idiots and of idiotic moments that are in all of us, but actually never happens, because it is intrinsically impossible, failing with the stimulus of practice both the subject and the purpose of knowing. And those intellectuals who advocate as the way to salvation the detachment of the artist or the thinker from the world that surrounds them, in their deliberate non-participation in the vulgar practical conflicts – vulgar because practical – do not realize that they are only advocating the death of the intellect. In a utopia where there is no work or labour, where there are no obstacles to overcome, one no longer thinks, because there is no reason to think, and one does not even contemplate, because active and poetic contemplations contain within themselves a world of practical struggles and affects.

Nor is it hard to demonstrate that even what we call the natural sciences, with their complement and instrument, mathematics, are based on the practical necessities of life and aim at satisfying them; this idea was instilled in the soul by its great advocate at the dawn of modernity, Sir Francis Bacon. But at what point of their process do the natural sciences exercise this useful task by truly becoming knowledge? Certainly not when they create abstractions, construct classes, establish relations among classes that they call laws, and give mathematical formulas to these laws, and so on. All these approaches aim at preserving the already acquired knowledge or at finding new ones, but they are not the act of knowing. One can possess the entire medical know-how in books or in memory, all the species and subspecies of diseases with all their characteristics, and thus being in possession of *"bien Galien, mais nullement le malade,"* as Montaigne would say, one will know as much or as little, or nothing at all, of history as do those who are acquainted with the many universal histories that have been compiled or stored in memory until the moment that, under the stimulus of events, those cognitions undo their static rigidity, and thought thinks a political situation or other. Similarly, an expert in medicine [does not know] until the moment he sees a sick man and he intuits and understands the disease, which only that patient suffers, in that way and in those conditions, which is no longer the outline of a disease but is its concrete and individual reality. Natural sciences move from individual cases, which the mind does not yet understand or understand fully, and undertake the long and complicated series of works to bring the mind, so trained, before those cases, in order to leave it in direct communication with them so that it can form a proper judgment.

There is really no conflict or opposition between the theory that every genuine knowledge is historical knowledge, and the natural sciences that, similarly to history, perform in the world and in the lower world – only philosophy, if you wish, the traditional idea of philosophy whose eyes are turned up to heaven and that from heaven expects or obtains the supreme truth. This division of heaven and earth, this dual conception of a reality that transcends reality, of a metaphysics on physics, this contemplation of the concept outside judgment or without it, gives it its own characteristic, which is always the same, independently of how one chooses to name transcendental reality – God, Matter, Idea, or Will – as long as one supposes that an inferior or a merely phenomenal reality stands below it or against it.

But historical thought has played a joke on this respectable transcendental philosophy and on its sister, transcendental religion, of which it is the reasoned or theological counterpart. The joke is to historicize it by interpreting all its concepts and doctrines, arguments, and disheartened sceptical renunciations as historical facts and historical statements borne out of certain needs that are left partly satisfied and unsatisfied. In so doing, historical thought gave them their due, which they deserved because of their long domination (which was at the same time their service to human society), and wrote their honest obituary.

We could say that with the historical critique of transcendental philosophy, philosophy itself, in its autonomy, is dead, because its claim to autonomy was based precisely on its metaphysical character. What took its place is no longer philosophy but history or, which is the same, philosophy as history, and history as philosophy – philosophy-history that has as its principle the identity of the universal and the individual, intellect and intuition, and declares as arbitrary or illegitimate any separation of the two elements, which in reality are only one. It is a peculiar occurrence of history, which has long been considered and treated as the most humble form of knowledge, and, by contrast, philosophy as the highest [form], and now it seems that [history] not only has gone beyond the latter but is driving it away. However, the so-called history, which was confined to last place, was not really history but chronicle or erudition and was confined to the margins, working on documentations. The other, which has risen now, is historical thought: the sole and integral form of knowledge. When the old metaphysical philosophy wanted to give a helping hand to history to sustain it, it did not offer that hand to history but to chronicle, and because it could not raise it to history because it was barred by its metaphysical character, it imposed on it a "philosophy of history," namely, that form of contrivance or guess-work, which we discussed earlier, concerning the divine program that history presumably performs, similar to those who try to copy a model more or less well. The "philosophy of history" was the result of a mental impotence or, to say it with Vico, of a "lack" (inopia) of the mind, similar to myth.

To be sure, among the many literary forms of allegory [didascalia] there are examples that are taken to be philosophical and not historical because they seem to deal with abstract concepts, devoid of any intuitive element. But if those treatises do not dwell in the void, if they have fullness and concreteness of judgment, the intuitive element is always there, even though it is invisible to common perception, which believes that it recognizes it only when it appears as the encrustation of chronicle or erudition. The intuitive element is there for the simple reason that the sophisms that are formulated answer to the exigency of shedding light on particular historical conditions, and their knowledge brightens them as much as they are brightened by it. I was about to say, by providing an example from life, that even the methodological clarifications that I have been giving are only intelligible by rendering mentally explicit the reference (which I usually have rendered only implicitly) to the political, moral, and intellectual conditions of our time, whose description and judgment they contribute.

The task of the specialists or the professors of philosophy seems to counter that of the philologists, that is, the scholars who pretend to be historians, by placing next to the brute facts, which they organize and pass for history, an alignment of abstract ideas, thus covering one's ignorance with another's, which does not take us very far. They are the natural keepers of transcendental philosophy to the extent that, even when they profess with words the unity of philosophy and history, they disclaim it with facts, or, at most, they come down from their pedestals to utter some outdated generality or some historical falsehood. But the more our own sense of history is sharpened and the historical mode of thinking is spread, the historian-philologist will revert back to pure and simple and useful philology, and the professional philosopher will be politely thanked and dismissed because philology has discovered in high historiography the condition of active life that they had looked for in vain. They philosophized coldly, without stimulus of passion or interest, "without occasion," whereas any serious historiography and any serious philosophy must be a historiography-philosophy "of occasion," just as Goethe used to say about genuine poetry: one passionately and the other practically and morally, motivated.

The Concept of History as Absolute Historicism

(*Il carattere della filosofia moderna*, chap. 1, pp. 9–28)

[9] I would like to summarize briefly my discussion, by emphasizing all the essential links and passages, supplemented by necessary historical references, of the reasons why I believe that the resolution of philosophy in historiography, "absolute historicism" is, to coin a phrase by Bacon, "*temporis partus masculus*," the mature product of the development of the history of thought to the present day. The reason that this birth has come to light now and not before, that it could come to fruition now and not before, depends on the fact that only in the nineteenth century did thought bring to conclusion a series of logical assumptions that were necessary and imprint the seal of necessity on its free action, without making it possible to continue or to return to different conceptions unless one chose to remain idly under the weight of old traditional ideas.

For the sake of exposition I would like to divide my thesis into two parts: first, that philosophy is nothing else, nor ever was, but philosophy of the Spirit; second, that the philosophy of Spirit cannot be concretely, and actually never was, other than historical or historiographical thought, in whose process it represents the historically conditioned moment of methodological reflection, to which one can give greater or lesser importance by making it the object of a particular literary or didactic treatise, but which is inseparable intrinsically from the single process.

In the history of philosophy, which is also the history of thought, we observe the conflict and the various and ceaseless struggles of critical knowledge or philosophy of the Spirit against two opposite ways of providing the soul with the light of truth it requires. The first one of these ways is not, as it seemed to Plato, poetry, which in its ingenuity neither fights against thought nor is fought by it, but is myth or the revealed truth of religions. Unlike poetry, which is simple ideal or lyrical image, myth is an image that acts as conceptual truth, as explication of things and events, and therefore is philosophically inconceivable and indemonstrable, but nonetheless believable in the presumption that it carries within itself, based on the testimony of dreams, visions, oracles, facts creatively interpreted, misunderstood phrases of deluded or deceitful seers and on the authority of tradition that keeps it and holds it sacred, while theology, the intense logical and doctrinal activity, situates it and reasons, but only to the limits of revelation, that in the last instance one must revere it and accept it. The second way, which follows this one and takes its place or stands alongside it, is metaphysics, the nature of which we must better define.

Metaphysics is created by the separation of myth from revealed truth in the search for categories in which to think reality, when the mind, once it has begun the motion of separation and research, still not finding its proper way, tries to adhere to the method of the natural or empirical sciences, which are the sciences that most properly suggest a model that is no longer mythic but scientific. Hence, its attempt to devise beings that are at the same time philosophical concepts, empirical concepts that are at the same time pure concepts, objects or material forces that are at the same time spiritual and logical, trying to think these figures or mental combinations that are not really thinkable, because they are hybrid [...]

[21] In the second half of the twentieth century, philosophy was idle, in conditions so weak and poor that, with hardly an awareness of itself, it was forgotten by the next and best traditions – between scientism, naturalism, and related metaphysics – and denied in words but introduced surreptitiously and actually upheld in fact. Precisely in this tradition, and especially in the treasures that Hegel's thought had locked under its metaphysical armour, and which should have been pulled out of there, it could have stood upright and used two refutations but it did not know how, which would have allowed it to abolish the obstacles that were still in its way and that prevented it from being acknowledged and determined, and defined as philosophy of the Spirit, as total philosophy. Those obstacles consisted mainly of a dual but joint dualism: the dualism of internal and external reality, of body and soul; and the dualism of values, of Being and non-Being, of life and death, of good and evil, or of any other type. Any time that the inner life of the Spirit believes that it is confronting something external – the body, matter, the object – it feels forced to admit a second reality, a *res extensa*, which is obedient to laws that are not its own and that the natural sciences discover, and thus the necessity of a transcendental unity that embraces them. Similarly, as long as the good, the beautiful, the true, and life are opposed to evil, the ugly, falsehood, and death, which are as real as they are, we are led to postulate a world of values outside and above the two opposing series, free of their antinomies, a world of pure truth, goodness, and beauty, a world of a pure life without death, and thus to imagine a transcendence. But Hegel's thought, gathering and bringing to the highest energy the efforts of previous philosophers, conquered this duality of opposites with a dialectic and established their unity, demonstrating that the separation of Being from non-Being was nothing more than an abstraction and an arbitrary act of the intellect; and he showed that divisions were equally abstract and

arbitrary, so that the terms of the real are placed one outside the other. Thus the second term of those dualisms was welded together with the first, which in this way, once the abstractions had been dispelled, acquired its own concreteness. The principle of contradiction of the old logic, which denied that a thing both is and is not at the same time, was replaced by a higher principle of contradiction that proved the other to be contradictory and inadequate [...]

[24] On the other hand, if those two orders of truth have appeared theoretically separate or just parallel, they still allow in their actual course a glimpse of the connection between them, or a first form of unification. If one looks closely, historiography in every age always depends more or less directly on the contemporary conditions of thought, and in its narratives and explanations of facts and events it is possible to find the concepts and also the limitations and the errors that belong to the contemporary philosophy of Spirit, all the opacity caused by presumed metaphysical entities, all the disruption brought about by the obstinacy of religious myths, together with the light of criticism that clarifies and replaces them. Only with this thread is it possible to understand the history of historiography from its most ancient and poorest manifestations because we must be wary of believing that philosophy intervened only when, as it did in the eighteenth century, its name resounded and when in the new century it exercised its power and arrogance. The same "historical sense," which seemed that one had acquired for the first time, was only an addition, a sharpening, and a refinement of the philosophical concepts formed not only in the minds of individual philosophers but in the philosophies of specific historiographers.

Nonetheless, by understanding the relation of philosophy and history as that of guide and guided, light and lighted, form and matter, one must not hide the fact that a form of transcendence persists or is reproduced with a kind of superiority towards history, as a sovereign is to its subject, not unlike that of metaphysical beings towards the reality of experience. In order not to fall into the error of representing the spirit as a metaphysical and transcendental being, there is no other way than to conceive philosophy as equally dependent on history as history is dependent on philosophy. And since neither Spirit nor history is a naturalistic concept, their reciprocal dependence cannot be thought in the naturalistic way of reciprocal action but only in the form of a synthetic or dialectical unity.

This statement of the unity of history and philosophy refers back to Hegel, usually to refute it, but to be fair to him we only find it in the formula of the unity of philosophy with its history, and even here not in a real, proper, and actual identification of one to the other, but rather as a doubling of the philosophical process, first thought in idea and then found in historical reality, in which the eternal categories are temporalized and follow one another as chronological epochs, each appropriate to its given epoch – hence the reasonable revolt of historians against this treatment of history as a reduction to an allegory of a doctrinal truth. There was indeed in Hegel and Kant a concept that, if developed and studied, would lead one to find and to establish the true and proper unity: in Kant we find, for instance, the synthesis a priori of concept and intuition that, if one ever tried to separate them, the first would become empty and the second blind; in Hegel we find a new formulation of the synthesis a priori – the new concept of the concept or the idea as the unity of logos and representation, of the universal and the individual. But Kant, all absorbed by the problem of the physical sciences, did not really have a sense of the problems of history; and Hegel, though he initially identified the rational with the real, separated them again by allowing the irrational and the arbitrary to remain almost as the dross of the real; and, even though he wrote that philosophy is the spirit of an epoch that thinks itself, he never investigated the proper historical quality of philosophy, which is to be referred to not as the abstract and generic character of an epoch but as the individual, passionate, and moral stimulus that is always in everyone who thinks and that makes him think. If he had done that, the history of philosophy would have taken a more varied and rich progression, and he would have freed himself of the metaphysically religious preconceptions of an "eternal gospel" that still weighed on him to announce to all men a final and definitive philosophy.

Therefore, the proof of the unity of philosophy and history must be understood and worked out in another way. Once it has been posited that historical judgment is the unity of individual and universal, subject and predicate, representation and concept, one has to show that there is no genuine and concrete judgment that is not also historical, and that historical are also the solutions and the definitions of philosophy, which always refer to the particular historical situations in which the thinker finds himself from time to time. These situations, in giving origin to the correlative problem of knowledge by the very act of their solution and definition, are historiographically illuminated, represented, and judged. True philosophy, very differently from the colourless treatises and dissertations of the schools, is full of the passionate and moral life that it gathers within itself, whose needs it satisfies by removing the mental obscurities that trouble it and by placing before them the historical situation in its truth, thus preparing the further satisfaction that is practical action. Far from feeding on a sterile contemplation and adoration of the divine life of the universe – as fanatics and rhetoricians describe it and extol it, who also make use of it for their proofs – or far from being a liberation from the labours of life, philosophy works by taking part in the continued creation of an always new world. To this logical statement corresponds the history of philosophy in which, on the one hand, there is no concept or doctrine that has not been involved in life and, on the other hand, there is nothing intelligible unless the affections and the practical needs of the various ages are made present – or, rather, of the single thinkers in various periods of their experience and passionate life, both practical and moral. Thus the first rule when interpreting a philosophical proposition is to ask against whom or against what one is turning polemically, and what "anguish" it has overcome or it has tried to overcome. Outside of this serious historical interpretation even the theories of philosophers take on, similarly to metaphysical systems, the aspect of a series of empty assertions, in conflict with one another, as they seem in fact to the uninitiated, those who do not think by rethinking them. Scepticism sits on the pile of their ruins, laughing its inane laughter.

Thus, once philosophy has been intrinsically and solidly unified with historiography, and the Spirit with its history, what becomes thinkable and can alone be thought is the individuality of actions that are not to be transcended, even by thinking the Spirit in and for itself, because, as we said, the Spirit is never in and for itself but is always historical. And although didactic treatises of so-called pure philosophy are being written and have to be written, that is, definitions and systems of spiritual categories, and even though these treatises may appear general and abstract, and void of any historical reference, they are always rooted in historical ground, and the historical lymph rises through their veins. The reduction of didactic philosophy to a "methodology of historiography" (according to the definition that I proposed many years ago) closes the way to a possible metaphysical misunderstanding of the philosophy of Spirit and of the absolute Spirit and confers on it the more fitting name of "absolute historicism."

Literary Criticism

Our selection is a small sample of Croce's vast production in the field
of literary criticism, but it aims to address some of the key issues discussed in the other sections as they relate to literary criticism. The first
selection, on Dante, addresses the question of allegory. The selection
on Ariosto's harmony addresses the issue of irony, and the selection on
Pirandello addresses the question of the distinction between art and
philosophy, as well as the issue of humour or irony. In the excerpt from
La poesia di Dante at issue is the relation of poetry and structure, poetry
and prose or the prosaic – or, which is the same, symbol and allegory.
In his analysis of Dante's *Commedia*, Croce attempts to isolate pure
poetry from the structure that stands for everything that is non-poetic
or rhetorical. He also makes the case for the inseparability of poetry and
structure, of the theological novel and the lyrical poem in Dante, since
they are "inseparable parts of his soul." They condition one another,
and in this dialectical sense they form the unity of the *Commedia*.

In the essay on Ariosto, irony is criticized for being detrimental and
destructive of art. Croce prefers to call it "harmony," a notion that does
not have the negative connotations of irony and implies a principle of
preservation: "we must understand it as destruction in the philosophical sense, which is also preservation." He compares the process to the
technique in painting of "veiling a colour" (velare un colore), which
does not mean doing away with it, as in the case of irony, but "toning
it down" (smorzarlo). "In this equal toning down, all the feelings that
make up the plot of the poem keep not only their own physiognomy
but also their reciprocal proportions and relations." Croce's dislike of
irony is associated with the concept of "umorismo" (humour), which
refers not only to the theories of irony of the German Romantics, and

mainly to those of Friedrich Schlegel, but also to Pirandello's theory of irony.

The essay on Pirandello is a critique of his novels and plays that aims primarily to criticize the author's tendency to philosophize, or pseudo-philosophize, as Croce calls it, that is, to universalize the everyday problems of his characters into a universal dilemma. Pirandello's work raises the issue of the relation of art and philosophy, which are not dealt with as separate or distinct concepts, as Croce would like, but are confused with one another, with the result that a work of literature is open to the interference of metaphorical or rhetorical language, over which the critic has no control. This flaw causes an "anguish" similar to that of the philosopher, which Croce resolves, as I have indicated, by attributing the error not to rhetorical language but to the personal shortcomings of Hegel and Vico. In this case, the shortcomings are Pirandello's. Croce urges us to always be on guard against the detrimental effects of metaphors, but he also shows that even a clear and rigorous mind like his does not have the "presence of mind" to be vigilant over his own language and to know when he is being interfered with. This is Croce's anguish but also the lesson that he teaches us today and that *A Croce Reader* brings to its readers.

The Structure of the *Commedia* and Poetry
(*La poesia di Dante*, chap. 2, pp. 58–68)

[58] About the structure of the *Commedia*, that is, the theological novel that serves as its foundation, has risen one of the most conspicuous sections of Dante criticism that for its volume competes with that devoted to allegory; this is criticism of the "physical topography" and the "moral topography" of the three reigns [...] [58] Thus it is a waste of time and bothersome to discuss and to hear whether Dante took seven, nine, or ten days in his journey, and whether he spent twenty-eight, forty-two, or seventy-two hours in Paradiso, and whether he went up there before or after midday, and so on. But Dante scholars force us to repeat on this point the other critique regarding the non-methodological character of their analyses and to explain of what it consists. Even though Dante was careful and meticulous, he left some lacunas (vuoti) in the workings of his theological novel, and even though he was careful, he ran into some contradictions, perhaps because, as some think, he was not able to have a last look at his poem and to reorganize a work

that was composed over many years and under the pressure of many and different events. If his work had been philosophical or critical, one could have easily filled the spots and resolved the contradictions, as we do when we study philosophers, picking up and continuing their investigation and drawing the logical consequences that derive from their propositions. But since it is a work of the imagination, and since what he did not say also belongs to the imagination, we cannot logically compensate or reconcile what has been contradicted unless we also want to use our imagination, which, without the good reasons that motivated Dante, would entail conjecturing. As usual, Dante scholars are not aware of this logical impossibility, hence the debate on how Dante went from one shore of Acheron to the other; where the souls of the children in Limbo go after the Last Judgment, as well as those of the virtuous pagans, and whether they will be given as final resting place the "divine forest" of the Earthly Paradise; why Cato is the guardian of Purgatory when he died half a century before Purgatory was even instituted, so one is made to believe that he was in Limbo before, but then, because he seems not to know Virgil who also was in Limbo, this leads us to think that there are various circles or clubs in Limbo and that Virgil and Cato belong to different clubs or that in the centuries that Cato was in Purgatory he forgot the shape and the language of his old countryman. Or what happens to Cato after the Last Judgment, whether he goes back to Limbo or up to Heaven where he can find a seat, and so on and so forth with similar "Dantesque questions" that are resolved in much the same way and about which it is best to keep silent.

What is worse, there is a prejudice, a preconceived idea in all this passion for research on the physical and moral topography of the three kingdoms, that this type of information concurs in determining, and in making one understand and appreciate Dante's art, the character of the three cantiche and the reasons for the passage from one to the other, from one episode to the next – hence the story of the otherworld conceived as an aesthetic history and the relations and the devices as artistic subtleties. But since the structure that we have briefly outlined derives not from a poetic impulse but from a didactic and practical intention, it is no use to point out either the particular poetic character, if there is one, or the passages from one cantica to the other. It can only provide what is in its nature, namely, connections that are extrinsic to poetry and determined by structural reasons. Every effort to convert these reasons into aesthetic reasons is sterile, a waste of intelligence. The poetry of the three cantiche cannot be deduced from the concept of the journey through the three kingdoms by which means humanity, and Dante who represents it, passes from the anguish and guilt for its sins to repentance and purgation, and beyond to the beatitude or moral perfection. This is one of the aspects of the theological novel but not the main principle of the poetry that adheres to it. The beautiful representation of Venice's Arsenal does not find its place and its poetic justification in the asserted intention that, as it has been quibbled, Dante wanted to compare the spectacle of a fervent economic activity to the evil bustling of the barrators; or that Virgil's excursus on the origins of Mantua gives an example of true history in contrast to the tall tales of witches and wizards; or that Ulysses, who tells of his last heroic travels as explorer, has anything to do with the fraudulent among whom he is condemned. Each of these episodes exists by itself and is a lyric by itself, and we cannot even consider the structure that supports the poetry as the "technical part" of the poem, because the technique (as we should admit by now) either does not exist in art or coincides with art itself, whereas the structure of the *Commedia*, because it has a different psychological origin, does not quite coincide with the poetry.

This structure has been compared, with greater accuracy, to a picture frame that encloses one or more paintings, even though this image runs the risk of giving it a more properly aesthetic virtue because frames are usually created together with paintings or artistically worked in such a way as to form a harmony, almost to complement the paintings, which is not really true in this case. One could represent it rather as a robust and massive factory over which a luxuriant vegetation climbs and extends, adorned with hanging branches, festoons, and flowers, covering it in such a way that only here and there some piece of the unrefined stonework or some corner of its hard lines shows up. But, metaphors aside, the relationship with poetry is simply the one that passes between a theological novel, that is, a didactic poem, and the lyric that gives it variety and interrupts it continuously. This relation is comparable to that of other poetic works and above all to Goethe's *Faust*, which has been often compared to the *Commedia* for historical reasons (one as a synthesis of medieval thought and feeling, and the other as a synthesis of the modern age), but also for artistic reasons (though the two works are very different) because beyond their poetry they both have a bond among their parts that is somewhat extrinsic and conceptual or didactic. (See my study on Goethe's *Faust*).

It cannot be denied that the theological novel exerts a certain pressure over the poetic vein, as we can see in some cases. This is due to

the necessity of inserting merely informative parts, or allegorical hiero-
glyphs, which do not require special examples. Such is the breakdown
of the coherence whereby characters and scenes, which have their own
emotional and sentimental value, are then forced to serve as expedients
to provide information or some doctrinal explanation [...] [63] And,
finally, in brief, that same pressure is responsible for the way in which
certain scenes and dialogues conclude in a very brusque and firm
way (hence the joke that Dante's characters take their leave without
compliments, "English style," or, more seriously, that Dante "imprints
his brand on the characters' forehead and moves on"). In general, it
could be said that because of the measures imposed on the structure
of the theological novel, because of art's restraint [lo fren dell'arte], the
Inferno is overcrowded, sometimes to the choking point, and the Paradiso is a bit too extended.

On the other hand, we should be reminded of the freedom that the
otherworldly and encyclopedic structure allows to the most varied
movements of Dante's imagination. We should also note the beneficial
effects that the pressure exercises, whereby Dante's poetry acquires a
characteristic of absolute necessity, by breaking through the structure
that has been rendered more vigorous and intense by the obstacles that
have been interposed on it and that it overcomes. So that, to those who
do not believe in the reality and in the necessity of poetic production
(and there are many sceptics) and who consider it to be a play or an
artifice that man could do without, one could not offer a better proof on
which to reflect than the poetic furor in Dante the theologian and the
politician, this torrent forced by the poetic vein, which opens its way
among the rocks and the stones and flows impetuously. Its power is so
great, as is its wealth, that it penetrates every cave of rock and stone and
envelops them with its foamy waves and with the veil of water that lifts
the alpine scenery to such a degree that often one cannot see anything
else but the movement of its waters. Dante's poetry, when it cannot
do anything else, animates with fresh imagination the particular arguments, the informative parts, and the devices of the narrative, and even
the frequent conceits of Dante's erudition in history, mythology, and
astronomy, and invests all these with his emotional and sublime accent.

For these reasons the poetry and the structure, the theological novel
and the lyric, cannot be separated in Dante's poem, just as the parts of
his soul cannot be separated, where one conditions the other and thus
flows into the other, and in this dialectical sense the *Commedia* is certainly
a unity. But those who have eyes and ears for poetry will always discern,

throughout the poem, what is structural and what is poetic – to a greater extent than in other poets where we also find the same combinations, and perhaps, as we said, similar to Goethe's *Faust*, but almost entirely in opposition to Shakespeare's major plays where the scheme or the structure originates from a poetic impulse, and there is no structure and poetry, but everything, we could say, is homogeneous, everything is poetry [...]

[66] It should be clear by now how we should deal with the structural parts of the *Commedia*, which should not be taken to be pure poetry, not even rejected as bad poetry, but we should respect them as the practical necessities of Dante's spirit, and poetically pause on something else [...] [67] One must not insist on these [boring issues], but dwell on something else, that is, reading Dante precisely the way in which naive readers read him and are right to read him, paying little attention to the other world, very little to the moral subdivisions, and not at all to the allegories, and enjoying the poetic representations in which all his many-sided passions are condensed, purified, and expressed. People will say, and it has been said, that in this fashion Dante is being diminished, but the opposite is the case. What is being increased is his potential as poet [...] The real unity of Dante's poetry is in his poetic spirit, the spirit of Dante of the *Commedia* and not of his poem as a whole. The character of each of the three cantiche can be found not by analysing the concepts of the Inferno, Purgatory, and Paradise but only by contemplating the poetry found in each cantica that, in its variety, holds a certain physiognomy that distinguishes it. It is not any different than if the same poet had collected his poems by grouping them by theme in three books.

To determine Dante's poetic spirit, and its major traits, the shortest and the most appropriate way is to read through the three cantiche, making sure to review the major poems or the group of poems, their contents, and observing their rhythm and inspiration.

The Realization of Harmony in Ariosto
(*Ariosto, Shakespeare, e Corneille*, pp. 44–59)

[44] The first change that [particular sentiments] underwent as soon as they were touched by the harmony that sang deep in the breast of the poet [Ariosto] was revealed in the loss of autonomy, in the submission to a single master, in the fall from a whole to a part, from motive to occasion, from ends to means, in the death of all for the benefit of a new life.

The magical force that accomplishes this wonder is the tone of expression, the self-assured tone, soft, capable of being transformed in many guises and always charming, which traditional critics used to call his "air of self-confidence" and listed among the other "qualities" of Ariosto's "style"; not only does his style consist entirely of this tone of expression, but since style is nothing but the expression of the poet and his very soul, it consists entirely of Ariosto, of his harmonious singing.

By means of this expressive tone this work of devaluation and destruction is tangible in the preamble to each canto, in the reasoned digressions, in the interpolated observations, in the refrains, in the terminology employed, in the phrasing and periodization, and, above all, in the frequent comparisons that make up the poetic descriptions, which do not strengthen the emotions but dissipate them. It is tangible in the interruptions of the stories, sometimes in their most dramatic moments by means of easy shifts to other narratives of a different and usually opposite nature. Nonetheless, what is tangible, which can be rhetorically isolated and analysed, is only a small part of the whole, a small part of what is intangible, which runs as a subtle fluid and does not let itself be grasped by academic devices, but, being soul, relates to soul.

This tone, which has often been observed and named but never well defined, is Ariosto's irony. It has never been well defined, because it has usually been thought a kind of joke or a sneer that is similar to the way in which Ariosto used to describe the knights and adventures of chivalry. So it was restricted and materialized at the same time. What we must remember is that irony does not target a set of feelings, for example those of knights or priests, while sparing others, but it involves everyone, and therefore it is not a futile joke but something more important, something more clearly artistic and poetic: the victory of the fundamental principle over everything else.

All feelings, those sublime and playful, those tender and strong, the effusions of the heart and the ruses of the intellect, the reasoning of love, the encomiastic catalogues of names, the battle scenes and witticisms, are all equally lowered and elevated by irony. Over their equal fall rises the wonder of Ariosto's octave in *Orlando furioso*, which is a living thing in itself. An octave that it would not be an exaggeration to call "smiling," if the smile is understood in the ideal sense to be the manifestation of a free and harmonious life, energetic and balanced, with good rich blood flowing in its veins. These octaves have the consistency of young women in bloom, of well-shaped youth, loose in the exercise of their movements, and who do not need to prove their deftness, because it is revealed in each posture and in each gesture. Olympia, after many misfortunes, after a long and stormy sea voyage, lands with her lover on a wild and deserted island:

> The travail of the voyage and the fear
> That for days had kept her awake,
> Finding herself on the beach now safe,
> Far from the noise, in the woods;
> And with no thought, or worry,
> Now that her lover was by her side, to bother her;
> These were the reasons that Olympia fell into such a great sleep,
> That bears and dormice could not sleep longer.
>
> (*OF*, X, 18)

We have here the complete analysis of the precise reasons that Olympia falls asleep, but all this is clearly secondary to the close feeling expressed by the octave that seems to be satisfied with itself as the result of a movement, a becoming that has reached its fulfilment. Bradamante and Marfisa together pursue King Agramante to kill him, in vain:

> As two beautiful and generous leopards
> Who out of the leash have both come out,
> After the deer and the lusty goats
> They had pursued in vain
> Almost ashamed that they were late,
> Disdainful and contrite they returned;
> Thus the two young women came back when
> They saw the Pagan safe, sighing.
>
> (*OF*, XXXIX, 69)

Same process, same result. But the same process and the same result can be observed even when there does not seem to be an intrinsic interest in the subject, that is, only a conventional idea and a ceremonious sentence as a courteous homage or a statement of esteem or friendship. To say of a beautiful woman that "she seems in every act a goddess descended from Heaven" is not an unusual saying, but Ariosto turns it around and rhymes it in such a way that we are witness to the revelation of a goddess at her majestic gate, to the astonished and devout kneeling of the people present and of her rivals, to the unfolding of a little drama:

Julia Gonzaga who wherever her foot
Steps and wherever her serene eyes she moves,
No other beauty can yield to her in beauty,
But, as a Goddess come from Heaven, they admire her.

(*OF*, XLVI, 8)

Reeling off just a list of names to remember them in praise, and changing some with a trite play on words, is even less unusual, but Ariosto makes use of the name of contemporary artists, as on Parnassus, to celebrate the greatest among them, and each of those bare names resounds in such a way (by a masterful use of punctuation and accent) that it seems as if they come alive and are full of sense:

And those who were in our day, or they are now
Leonardo, Andrea Mantegna, Gian Bellino,
two Dossi, and the one who equally sculpts and paints,
Michel, more than a mortal, a Divine angel.

(*OF*, XXXIII, 2)

Francesco De Sanctis judged Ariosto's maxims [sentenze] to be "commonplace" and "observations neither profound nor original," and even "banal" and "contradictory." But they are maxims by Ariosto, and before them we do not reflect but we sing:

Oh, great conflict in youthful thoughts,
Desire for praise, and love impulse!
Nor those who ponder more, will find the truth,
Which is superior, this or that?

(*OF*, XXV, 1)

Even in the riskiest places, where others would have fallen completely into lewd gratification, he succeeds in lowering and in raising the subject matter at the same time, as in Ricciardetto and Fiordispina's tale:

Neither the noise of drums nor the sound of trumpets
Were at the start of love's assault;
But kisses that imitated doves
Gave a sign to either go forward or to ascend.

(*OF*, XXV, 68)

One could say that Ariosto's irony is like the eyes of God, who observes the movement of creation, loving it equally, in good or ill, in the greatest parts as in the smallest, in man and in the grain of sand, because He made it all, only seizing in it the movement, the eternal dialectic, the rhythm, and the harmony. So, from the common use of the term "irony" we have moved to the metaphysical meaning that it had in Fichte and the Romantics, with whose theories we would very gladly explain the nature of Ariosto's inspiration if those thinkers and literary men had not confused irony with the so-called humour [umorismo], and with eccentricity and extravagance, that is, with attitudes that upset and disrupt art. However, the critical determination that we propose keeps itself rigorously within the boundaries of art, as in fact Ariosto did, who never lapsed into humour and the bizarre, a sign of weakness, but ironized as an artist, confident of his own powers. And, as it happens, this is one of the reasons that Ariosto was never liked by the Italian Romantics, the so-called *scapigliati*, who preferred Rabelais and even Carlo Gozzi to him.

To weaken all types of feelings, to adjust them to this reduction, to take away their autonomy, to deprive them of their particular and proper spirit, is equivalent to converting the world of the spirit to the world of nature: an unreal world that exists only in so far as we posit it. In some respects, "nature" becomes the whole world for Ariosto, a designed and coloured surface full of glitter but without substance. Hence his way of looking at objects in all their aspects, as a naturalist observes every detail and describes them without being satisfied with a unique trait, which other great artists observe instead and point out, without passionate impatience and with resulting indifference. The figure of Saint John, as it is portrayed, might appear to be done in jest:

> Whose mantle is red, and white the small gown,
> That to milk and to red-lead one can contrast;
> His hair is white, and white is the jaw,
> And a thick beard that runs over the chest.

> (*OF*, XXXIV, 54)

But, after all, Ariosto employs the same method to describe the beauty of Olympia, forgetting her chastity that would require a different type of representation or, rather, some more clothing:

> Olympia's beauties were those
> That are very rare, and not only the forehead,

The eyes, the cheeks, and the hair were beautiful.
The mouth, the nose, the shoulders, and the throat.

(*OF*, XI, 67)

And even Medoro is described with the same method, Medoro whose devoted and fierce heart, whose youthful heroism, would have required perhaps less a look at the freshness of the adolescent and more an attention to those traits that revealed his boldness and his devotion:

Medoro had a rosy cheek,
And white and agreeable in his youthful age

(*OF*, XVIII, 166)

The many similarities between characters and their situations, and scenes from the life of animals and the phenomena of nature, are also part of this almost graspable and tangible conversion of the human world into the world of nature. I will not give the statistics here, because a German philologist has already done that in a big volume that takes the fun away from even wanting to look, even for a moment, into these similitudes, comparisons, and metaphors [...]

[53] There are two ways in which one must not read *Orlando furioso*. The first one is the way in which one reads a eurhythmic book of the highest moral level like Manzoni's *I Promessi sposi* [*The Betrothed*], namely, by following throughout it the process of a serious human affection that moves in all its smallest parts, describing them and determining them all. The second way is the method that one adopts in reading a work like *Faust* in which the general narrative, more or less guided by mental processes, does not coincide at all with the poetic inspiration of the single parts, and in which it is best to differentiate poetic parts from non-poetic ones, and the poetically minded reader will bypass the latter and linger on the former and enjoy them. In *Orlando furioso* we do not find the imbalance, or very little, that is found in the second type of work, but we find instead the balance of the first type. However, it lacks the particular form of passionate seriousness that we find in every part of the first type and in a few parts of the second. Thus, *Orlando furioso* must be read in a third way: by following, beside the specific narratives and descriptions, a content that is always the same and realized always in new forms, and which attracts us with the magic of this sameness and, at the same time, with an inexhaustible variety of appearances [...]

[55] Ariosto's heart is isolated from the emotions that we usually associate with life and reality, but it is not separate, alien, or indifferent. On this score it is important to warn the reader against an easy misunderstanding of the "destruction," which we mentioned earlier, almost a total destruction and annihilation that is brought about by his tone and his irony; we must understand it as a destruction in the philosophical sense, which is also a preservation [...]

[57] The process of "destruction" of the subject matter could perhaps be made clearer, to those who do not have a taste for philosophical formulas or who find them too difficult, by means of a comparison with a technique that in painting is called "veiling a colour" [velare un colore], which means not erasing it but "toning it down" [smorzarlo]. In this equal toning down, all the feelings that make up the plot of the poem keep not only their own physiognomy but also their reciprocal proportions and relations [...]

[59] In defining Ariosto the poet of harmony we meant to indicate where the emphasis should be placed in his work, because he is the poet of a harmony that unfolds in a very particular world of feelings; in short, his harmony is not harmony in general but Ariosto's harmony.

Luigi Pirandello
(La letteratura della nuova Italia, vol. 6, pp. 357–70)

[357] When we speak of Pirandello and of his art, we always refer to the second type that consists of his theatrical works that he referred to as *Maschere Nude* [Naked masks] and of his novels of similar inspiration such as *Il fu Mattia Pascal* [*The Late Mattia Pascal*]. If I had to define in a few words of what this second manner consists I would say: a few artistic ideas, stifled or disfigured by a spasmodic, inconclusive philosophizing. It is neither genuine art nor philosophy, because it is prevented by an original flaw from developing according to either. Hence the surprising and disconcerting aspects with which it presents itself, and the debates that it provokes, and the hermeneutic quibbling, and the persistent uncertainty, and the void that seems full, and the full that feels empty, and, finally, in the readers or in the spectators, a dissatisfaction and an irritation that are so much the greater because the author does not lack intelligence, dialectic vivacity, and eloquence and possesses at times even a flash of affection and poetry.

In "L'umorismo" ["On Humour"] a work written after *Il fu Mattia Pascal*, Pirandello tried to theorize and work out his new ideal of art by writing on humour and considering himself a humorist. He said that humour, differently from the other arts, does not have feeling as its sole content, even though it is combined with an element of reflection, but the feeling is accompanied at every step by its opposite, the reflection that follows it as the shadow follows the body; thus, whereas non-humoristic art is preoccupied with the body alone, this art focuses also on the shadow, in fact more on the shadow than on the body (see my review in *Conversazioni critiche*, I, 44–48). But this kind of humoristic art is as inconceivable as it is non-existent, because if reflection accompanies the feeling, it remains distinct, just as criticism follows a poem step by step and therefore is distinct from the poem. If, however, it makes an effort to introduce itself in the feeling and into the imagination, the result, as one can imagine, is a bewilderment that is typical of Pirandello's second type.

I will explain my view with some examples; however, because it is not my aim to examine his novels and his plays one by one, I will begin by mentioning the best example of this second manner, the novel *Il fu Mattia Pascal*. It is the strange story of a man who, harassed by his wife, mother-in-law, debts, and other things, takes advantage of a misunderstanding that he has died by drowning, and does not return home, so that he can live and move freely in the world without obstacles. But soon afterwards he finds out that in order to move around without encountering irksome difficulties and insurmountable obstacles, he has to give proof of his personal identity from time to time: if he wants to launch a lawsuit for a theft received, to fight a duel, simply to deposit money in a bank, or just to marry the woman he loves and who loves him. Finally, he decides to fake another suicide, that of his second personality, and goes back to his home town, where he reacquires his lawful identity. Here there was enough subject matter for only a fine short story that could have had the title of "Il trionfo dello stato sociale" [The triumph of the welfare state], but Pirandello turns it into a long novel with a tone between wonder and anguish. The man who is dead but also alive, when he kisses the woman he loves, he wonders whether it is a dead man who is kissing her, a dead man who could never live for her. He behaves as if he were undergoing a tragic experience, and his problems reach complications that delve into the mystery of life.

These issues also arise expanded and central to his plays. Take for example, *Vestire gli ignudi* [*To Clothe the Naked*], which takes a pathetic situation as its starting point. After committing many mistakes a young woman tries to take her own life and, believing that she is close to dying, invents a story of the reasons that have led her to this point. She portrays herself as being innocent and betrayed, in order to give a sad and pure image of herself. She is cured and saved, but because her story has created much interest and commotion, her moving fiction falls apart bit by bit, and the ugly reality is exposed. She tries to kill herself again, and this time she succeeds, without the small dress with which she had tried to clothe herself. The desire of finding redemption in a fictional account becomes the argument for an open discussion on the theme that everyone feels the need to make a good impression on others [fare bella figura] and to circulate an image of oneself that is different from the real one, that is, to clothe one's nakedness with a dress made of lies. In this discussion the woman herself, who comes away from her death to go to her death, is not in the least eloquent, theoretical, or polemical. It would appear that even here some sad law of life is being revealed; however nothing is revealed because there is nothing to reveal [...]

[360] An initial motive of squalor, shame, and pity can also be found in one of his most renowned plays, Sei personaggi in cerca d'autore [Six characters in search of an author]. A widowed mother lives with her two daughters and with a son whom she had had by a previous husband. Now that the family lives in poverty, the oldest daughter is forced to prostitute herself. One day, as she is giving herself, she recognizes the man as her mother's first husband, and her stepfather, who now lives in another city and was in town by chance. When she was young, the man had loved her like a father and often accompanied her to school. The unexpected recognition in this base and tragic situation shatters everyone: the man, the stepdaughter, and the mother [...] [361] But the author is not interested in the story of these six characters. In fact, the drama that plays out is the life denied to these creatures by his imagination, a drama in which the author claims to represent no less than the creation of the artistic work! The six non-fully-realized characters present themselves, uninvited, on the stage of a theatre during rehearsal and ask the director and the actors to give them life. But between the six characters and the actors arises a conflict because the characters do not think that the actors are capable of representing them and their tragedy, because theirs is a fixed reality and that of the actors is a changing reality. But is there really a tragedy of art? Does it make any sense? What does it mean that an author denies his characters life? If they are his characters, if he has created them, he has given them life. One should rather say that they have not been fully realized, only sketched

or half-developed, or that they lack some necessary element that makes it impossible to portray them fully in language, in lines, in colours, and sounds? These things happen to every artist, to every thinker who has experienced these dark signs of art, of new and barely conceived concepts and judgments that they never succeeded either in bringing to completion or in forgetting. And what is the sense of accusing art of not adhering to reality? Perhaps because the purpose of art is to adhere and to repeat reality, and not, instead, to express solely the feelings of the artist on whose bases are formed figures, characters, actions – in short, a fantastic reality? The dialogue between the six characters and the actors is, for these reasons, so pointless that here and there, certainly against the intentions of the author, it takes on a tonality worthy more of a farce than of a tragedy.

A man kills himself because a woman betrayed him, but no one knows, not even the woman herself, if she betrayed him out of malice or to discourage him from the absurd marriage that he wanted to have with her. This is the subject of *Ciascuno a suo modo* [Each in his own way], which is not as new as it may seem, because the plot is similar to that of *La signora delle camelie* [The lady of the camellias] and her famous betrayal, out of goodness and generosity, that her lover misunderstands as malice. But even that theme, instead of being developed, is used to open a debate on the thesis that no one knows oneself, no one really can know either from oneself or from others what one really is, and everyone wavers in an idea of himself and of others according to his or others' imagination [...] [363] Why all this pathos, why all this noise for a discovery that is not a discovery? [...]

[363] I will not touch upon another of his most famous tragedies, *Enrico IV* [*Henry IV*], of which much has been debated already, which as a subject repeats the same theme of *Hamlet* – the madman who is not a madman or has ceased to be mad, and who has seen and understood all that has happened to him and that goes around him, and suddenly he breaks into a violent rage and takes his vengeance. I will just say that we get the usual philosophizing: Who is mad? Who is wise? Who knows others? [...] [364] All these statements have to do with the impossibility of knowing the truth, of going beyond appearances, which is also the theme of *Così è (se vi pare)* [*Right You Are (If You Think So)*]. A husband knows perfectly well that his wife is his second wife, whom he married after the death of his first one, whereas her mother, not any less perfectly, knows and sees that this second wife is always the first one, her daughter, who never died. In the meantime, due to earthquakes

and fires, all the documents have been destroyed that could have established which of the two in the placidity of their rhetoric is the madman.
The wife who could reveal the truth prefers not to because she does not
wish to destroy the illusion in which one of them lives. And this ironic
conviction could have been the focus of the work if the author had not
preferred, instead, to turn his work into a "parable" to illustrate the thesis that "the truth is what you think it is," a thesis that does not hold up,
certainly, to the fertile negativity of a Protagoras and of other sceptics
who came to philosophy to stimulate the progress of thought, but must
be called puerile once we admit that one of the two at least, because of
illness or shock, is mad [...]

[365] In Pirandello's *Trovarsi* [To find oneself] an actress returns to the
stage because she wants to find herself [...] [366] It seems to her that in
returning to the stage she has "found" herself, that she has found a new
balance, that she has conquered reality by being freed from reality [...]
As long as the observation concerning the frequency with which the
ideal personality of the actress ... tends to absorb the real one is kept
within its limits, it has a sense and a purpose. But when it is translated
in terms of a general problem, namely, if one finds oneself in life or
in art, what else can one say, without making much fuss, but that one
finds himself or herself in one aspect as in another? This is the case
not only with actresses or with theatre people but with every activity
(politics, economics, and even philosophy): there is a tendency to interfere [si profila la tendenza a interferire], on the strength of a particular
experience, with the conduct of the rest of one's life. For this reason
one ought to always keep watch over oneself [bisogna sempre vigilarsi]
and, in case, rouse oneself and become aware that what is now in front
of us, what we must do, is of a different nature from what we were
doing before.

With literary precedents in Ibsen's *When We Dead Awaken* or Poe's
The Oval Portrait, Pirandello's story *Diana e la Tuda* is not entirely new
in literature. It tells the story of a model who falls in love with the artist
for whom she poses and who sees only the model in her, only a practical instrument for his art. She believes, on the other hand, that the man
sucks the best of her being out of her and that she gives life and soul to
the work that he believes he takes from his own head. This anguish, as
usual, gets expanded theoretically to formulate an accusation that art
"fixes" what in life is flux and change. This is complicated by another
accusation to nature, by an old sculptor who observes with horror that
his body, which once had life and movement, is fixed in a form in which

life does not flow any longer, and, because he is unable to suffer the sight of this fixity, he destroys all the statues that by now have become hateful to him. We do not know what to say at this point except that art is frozen in a created form, just as much as it always creates new ones with the rhythm of any living thing, and that aging and death are precisely the passing of life from form to form.

Pirandello's last drama, *Quando si è qualcuno*, introduces us to one of Pirandello's most typical and delightful plays of the second type. This is the tragedy of a great man who feels that he is a prisoner of the judgment that would have him great, of the figure for which he is admired and fixed by his public, and he can no longer let himself go with the new impulses of life, of imagination, and of thought that arise in him; he is forced to stay as he once was and to remain like that for ever – no longer a living man but a monument of himself. This so-called tragedy is nothing but a misunderstood process of the human mind, which, not only in great men but in all men and all things, needs to form the so-called classifications that, however necessary, can be perverted and are frequently perverted by obstacles and prejudices towards the new judgments that are required by the new, which is always being produced. Therefore, individuals can feel themselves to be, according to circumstances, inferior or superior to the classification they have received, and which has a tendency to persist, and yet it must be, and it is, continuously modified or overturned. But if a single man or a great man imagines, like the protagonist of Pirandello's play, that he is a prisoner and suffers or dies because of it, in this case it is a question of puerile apprehension or mental inferiority, and it could result in a comic or pitiful representation, but never the one that Pirandello tries to give, heavy with an inexistent mystery and a mysterious tragedy [...]

[369] It seems to me that these examples sufficiently demonstrate the inconsistency of Pirandello's thesis [...] It is almost as if we found ourselves before Leopardi – not just the author of the *Idylls* but also Leopardi the polemist of the *Operette morali* who debates and with whom one debates – except that for Pirandello the poetic aspect is not pursued. To give an example, in the drama *Ciascuno a suo modo*, where it seems that in the characters and in their actions a sense of blindness, together with a sense of impurity, reigns continuously, not only do discussions and squabbles abound, but the old device of the theatre within the theatre is being employed. To the two acts on the stage two others alternate, where we see and hear the audience from the boxes and from the orchestra, and we observe the reactions and the exchanges between

what is represented on stage and what goes on in real life. This is called "Humour," but one would prefer to call it "facility of execution," and in this excessive facility is the origin of Pirandello's copious theatrical production; he has put together a recipe, has found a manner, which he employs with an air, with a style, which is not at all anguished, pained, and furious but at best the style of a driven intellectual who is himself a "prisoner" of the logical demons that he evokes and that he is unable to subdue and disperse.

The Baroque

In a note to the *History of the Baroque Age in Italy* (note B, 501–6) Croce outlines the aim of the work: to reverse the positive judgment that had been made of the seventeenth century in recent years and to restore it to its proper and original negative meaning. "The *History of the Baroque Age in Italy* represents, therefore, a conscious reaction to all those aspects of recent artistic and literary criticism and historiography that have taken pride in conferring a positive character on the concept of the Baroque, which was thought to be negative for a long time, and it still is by Jacob Burckhardt" (*Storia dell'età barocca in Italia* [*SEB*], 501).

Although he considers it to be a negative history, Croce undertakes to write the history of the Baroque because Italy, like Spain and Germany but unlike France and England, has made a significant contribution to this age that cannot be ignored. Croce limits himself to explaining in the introduction the concepts of Counter-Reformation, Baroque, and Decadence, and in the main part of the work he states what, according to Ranke, truly occurred (*was eigentlich gewesen*), that is, "what, even in its relative depression and decadence, and among the tumescence of the Baroque, Italy produced and accomplished" (*SEB*, 506). The *History of the Baroque Age in Italy* is really two histories: a history of the Baroque, as error that is relegated to the Introduction; and a history of what really occurred, which takes up the rest of the work proper and amounts to the history of what is negative about the Baroque which is a history of nothing, a history that was best left unwritten.

Although critics like René Wellek have later suggested that the term *baroque* comes from the Portuguese "*baroco*," Croce derived it from one of the terms of a syllogism, *Baroco*, which designates the fourth manner of the second figure. In so doing, Croce gave the Baroque not only its etymology but also its rhetorical origins as a trope, or as allegory. The Baroque as a pseudo-artistic form, as non-poetry, and as error defines the Baroque as allegory, as a prosaic form that is both ugly and cold, in the same way that Croce, after Hegel, defines allegory in the essay on allegory, as we have indicated in the section "Aesthetics."

Croce does not connect the Baroque to allegory directly. When discussing the theories of art in the seventeenth century, he states that the theory of art as allegory was still being practised. He quotes the example of Scipione Errico who, in the foreword to *La Babilonia distrutta* (Babylon destroyed), praised allegory as "the worthiest and rarest part of poetry ... without which poetic compositions, especially the greatest ones, would only be but an empty rumbling to fill the ears of the idle and the ignorant, and poetic art would be reduced to a low end if it were applied to pleasure alone as its ultimate end" (quoted in *SEB*, 169). This positive endorsement of allegory by Errico is followed by a condemnation of the use of allegory as an end in itself and just for pleasure. This is the sense in which Croce condemns it when he mentions cases in which allegory has become the "plaything of academics," or when Francesco Berni makes use of it to make fun in his satires. Croce condemns it outright, however, when Marino uses it in his *Adone* (*Adonis*), or when it is employed by his followers, with whom allegory "did not acquire seriousness" (*SEB*, 169–70). Croce also quotes some notable examples of criticism in the Renaissance made to Dante, in particular, whose allegory was preferred to the allegory of those who combined it with "civil action and religion" and "planted from the beginning a solid and real allegory," while Dante's is "just allegory" (allegoria sola) and "an airy or imaginary one" (170).

For Croce, the Baroque is strictly confined to the seventeenth century. The poetry of the sixteenth century, like Torquato Tasso's, appears to have been immune from it or, at least, capable of withstanding the pressure of allegory. Although Tasso was "the last great poetic voice of Italy" before the Baroque age, his great poem, *La Gerusalemme liberata* (*Jerusalem Delivered*), published in 1581, is not without its "weaknesses and flaws." Although the poem was written in the sixteenth century, some of its aspects can be said to "relate to the new age" (si lega bensí alla nuova età), that is, to the Baroque (*SEB*, 246). These secondary aspects, which Croce calls the "deaf parts" (le parti sorde), are the allegorical parts, the "more or less prosaic and structural," such as surveys, battle descriptions, and others that "are full of concepts and antitheses," and still others that are "not so much poetic sequences as rhetorical ones" (249). Despite these aspects, Tasso's poetry is sufficiently strong to withstand the blows of allegory and of the oncoming Baroque: "The impetuous poetry that moves it provides proof of its own strength in resisting, without receiving great damage, the obstinate literature and the incipient Baroque" (249). Although Tasso's *La Gerusalemme liberata* is afflicted by the same flaws and by the same errors as is baroque poetry, Tasso's poetry is pure enough and powerful enough to withstand the pressure of literature (or allegory) and of the Baroque in its initial stages. To demonstrate his point, Croce turns to his mentor Francesco De Sanctis for support: "De Sanctis said that when the situation is well devised [indovinata] in a work, everything is well devised." Croce modifies the statement to state that when "the substance is well devised, namely, poetic [substance], everything is forgiven – an easy forgiveness that great poetry usually needs." When we are dealing with great poetry, as in the case of Dante or even Ariosto, the prosaic or allegory can be easily forgotten or relegated to the margins. If an excuse is well devised, everything is well devised (250).

It is hard to know whether Croce was motivated by a desire to make Tasso's poetry appear, as much as possible, pure and free of allegory, or whether he wanted the pseudo-poetry of the Baroque to fall within the temporal line of the seventeenth century. The fact remains that the case of Tasso's *Gerusalemme liberata* demonstrates that every great poetry is also allegorical poetry. The definition of the Baroque as the artistic ugly – which takes the place of art, its appearance, and its name – is, after all, the result of an interference, of a "false and unhealthy element" (*SEB*, 181) that is added externally and generates a "fundamental ambiguity, oscillation, and hybridity" between art and non-art, between the pleasure of art and art as pleasure (182). This is what Croce finds in the theoretical statements and program of Giambattista Marino and the Marinisti: "a false and unhealthy element" that covers and submerges the pure and lyrical elements of poetry. "We have to please," Marino cried out, we must "titillate the ears of our readers with the oddness [bizzarria] of novelty." We must "adjust to the habits of the day and to the taste of the age" (182). The wonder that characterizes Marino's poetry is the wonder inherent in rhetorical language whose aim is not directed to producing any coherent meaning, but it is an end in itself, in the construction of a "coherent incoherence" (coerenza incoerente) that creates wonder. The art historian Alois Riegl, quoted by Croce, provides an example of this Baroque imagery that leaves one astonished: a dress that is violently moved by a hurricane while the leaves of a nearby tree are at rest. Why? "Why does the hurricane move the dress but not the leaves?" (29). The imagery defies explanation except to say that the baroque image is simply a rhetorical construct, an allegory that communicates wonder. It is not an allegory of something or a didactic exercise to allude to a meaning other than itself. On the contrary, allegory is itself that meaning, that wonder.

The Baroque is an age without poetry, where the great poetry is silent. After Tasso in the sixteenth century we have to wait until Romanticism for an age of great poetry (for Foscolo, Leopardi, and Manzoni) (*SEB*, 254). Between the two periods there are only two figures who qualify as poets, and they are both philosophers: Tommaso Campanella and Giambattista Vico. The poetry of Campanella remained hidden from the eyes of his contemporaries in a little book that only a few knew about and even fewer read, *La città del sole* (*The City of the Sun*), and Vico's "poetry," similarly, was "hidden" in the philosophy of the *Scienza nuova* (*New Science*). Croce is well aware that by claiming philosophers to be poets, he is crossing the line between philosophy and poetry, but he chides those who may accuse him of being unnecessarily traditional: "No," he writes, "for those who look to the reality of things and do not look at traditional classifications, great poetry gave signs of itself, at the time of Metastasio, in a philosopher, the heir of Campanella, the author of the *New Science*, who relived in thought the drama of budding humanity" (*SEB*, 254). In either case, however, it is a question not of blurring the lines between philosophy and poetry but of displacing them as philosophers. As I have already indicated in the section on Vico, Croce claims that the *New Science* is really a poetic work that foreshadows his own more scientific or philosophical work. The same goes for Campanella, who is described as a poet because his contribution as a philosopher is secondary. In Croce's view, neither Campanella nor Vico are philosophers; they are poet-philosophers, that is, philosophers who expressed themselves as poets through metaphors, as poets do, and not through concepts, so they cannot be considered philosophers in the modern and scientific sense of the term.

The example of Campanella points to another aspect that distinguishes him from the other poets of the seventeenth century, namely, that he expressed his "philosophy" poetically and not in prose or didactically: "Campanella, who laid out his metaphysics and cosmology in treatises, did not resort to didactic prose to express what he had in his chest but tended *to sing it* [a cantarlo]" (*SEB*, 251, my emphasis).

Campanella expressed his philosophy poetically or symbolically and not allegorically, as other Baroque poets or pseudo-poets like Marino and the Marinisti did.

Croce claims that there are no historical causes for the Baroque. It is an "aesthetic sin" (*SEB*, 33), an "artistic perversion" (34), a human error, and as such there are no causes, as there is no cause for the "sinful nature of man" (36). The Baroque seems to be an unexpected event that occurred between the sixteenth and the seventeenth century because there is nothing in the Renaissance or in previous ages to justify the presence of the Baroque age, its perversions, ugliness, and incoherence. There is only an end to the Baroque that coincides with the end of the seventeenth century so that the perverted and sinful nature of the Baroque is limited just to that century and ends with that century. Croce is especially thankful to the seventeenth century for having taken on the burden of allegory and for having dealt with it, once and for all, sparing other centuries: "to whom do we owe this clarity of judgment and determination of principles but to that age that took upon itself all the sins that could be committed and expiated them all? Even the Baroque age as baroque, then, did not live in vain" (42).

Although the style that dominated the seventeenth century can be said to be Baroque, whatever its etymological derivation, it becomes clear why the Baroque does not have a cause and why it is not a fact of history. Allegory is a rhetorical construct, an inscription, as Croce defines it in *La poesia*, the result of an interference on the part of the "impoetic," the prosaic, which always accompanies the poetic. In the seventeenth century this took the form of a hedonistic aesthetics that differed radically from previous forms. It is a materialistic aesthetics founded on the materiality of the sign, on the nothing of the rhetorical construct, which, as Croce points out, is really only a shell waiting to be filled with meaning.

Croce's complaint of the poetry of Giambattista Marino, who was hailed in his time as the greatest poet of the seventeenth century, is precisely that his poetry was a method, a formula, that could be learned and used by anyone, and that his poetry was "convoluted and pompous" and "made of nothing." "It contains many things and yet contains nothing, nothing poetic and nothing felt" (*SEB*, 258). The poetic process was the same for every poet; only the names changed, but not the quality of the poetry. The variety in ideas and combinations was so mechanical as to leave one indifferent (258). Croce compares Marino's poetic process to a "rich drapery" that can envelope any object, indifferent to the object itself" (272).

The *Storia dell'età barocca in Italia* is an instance of Croce's critique of allegory with his attempt at confining it to a single age, the seventeenth century, which alone is supposed to profess it and contain it. Any attempt to characterize poets of other centuries as Baroque, such as D'Annunzio, is misplaced because his poetry cannot be said to be affected, ideologically or historically, as Marino's poetry was: "all the similarities with Marino do not erase the fact that a D'Annunzio could only have arisen after Romanticism, Naturalism, Parnassianism, Nietzscheanism and other spiritual events that certainly did not precede Marino, because they came to maturity in the nineteenth century" (*SEB*, 35).

However, the impossibility of confining allegory to a single century becomes apparent when Croce's discussion of Marino's pseudo-poetry begins to echo the errors of another age and of another poetry that he had found similarly abhorrent and devoid of poetry, another negative history, a history of nothing that Croce never wanted to write, that of Futurism and Fascism. It is certainly uncanny, or baroque, that in speaking of the Baroque, Croce unwittingly refers to the futuristic poetics for which he had the same dislike as he had for Marino's. In speaking about aesthetic freedom, or the lack thereof, in the poetics of the Baroque, Croce compares the situation to the lack of freedom of his own day: "Instead of aesthetic freedom, in short, there was a freedom that today we would call 'futuristic'" (*SEB*, 184). Croce's contempt for Marino and the Marinisti becomes a contempt for Marinetti and his futurists, reinforced by the similarity in names, so that a critique of Marino's pseudo-poetics and poetry becomes a critique of Futurism and, by extension, of Fascism because Futurism was for Croce a child of the "irrationalism" of Fascism.

The analogy appears intended from the way that Croce goes out of his way to warn the reader that no analogy is intended: "we could say that, especially for his example and for his school [Marino's and Marinisti, respectively], 'verses were done well' [I versi si fecero bene], everywhere in Italy, *in that century*" (*SEB*, 272, italics mine). The statement is followed by another and more veiled critique when, in targeting the Marinisti, Croce speaks of their "ingenuity of aspiration ... which rests on the belief, *common to many today* [a molti ancor oggi comune], that into this empty beautiful shell one could eventually introduce a poetic content, or that it could be used to adorn a worthy poetic content (272, emphasis mine). Another veiled reference occurs when Croce refers to Marinisti as Marino's "followers" (seguaci), which does not really apply to Marino, who did not have a school, unlike Marinetti who drew up the "Futurist Manifesto" that was supposed to state the program of his poetic school.

The few statements we have from Croce on the poets of his time, as I discussed in the Introduction, match his attitude towards Marino and other baroque artists; so what is being said here about Marino is really meant for Marinetti: "your deliberate and manufactured 'lyricism' deserves another name, i.e., charlatanism and histrionics" (*Pagine sparse*, vol. I, 369; also quoted in Orsini, *Benedetto Croce*, 48). In another essay, on the Futurists, "Pensieri sull'arte dell'avvenire" (Thoughts on the art of the future), he wrote that Futurism is "extraneous to art" and that it is "not a form of poetry or art that one can discuss … but is actually and simply something that is neither poetry nor art" (*Storia d'Italia*, 272). Croce gives a reason why there is no point to writing about Futurism: "I study poetry, and that junk [roba] is something else" (272). Proof that the poetry of Futurism is worthless is that it has not entered the "imagination" or the "memory" of the public (274). As for the claim that Futurism is a school without a leader and without a masterpiece, this confirms him in the view that Futurism is a school of anything but art: "of anything else (perhaps car racing or aviation) but art" (274). Because Futurism is not art but chicanery and factionalism, there is no alternative but to wait for the momentary fad to pass: "And what is the remedy? There is none. We must wait for this evil to pass, for this epidemic that has attacked art to pass" (274).

It is in this context that Croce compares Futurism to "*secentismo*," the poetry of the seventeenth century: "History gives us a similar example of epidemic. In this case the classical example remains '*concettismo*' and '*secentismo*,' which imploded after seventy years of fever, during which it assumed more and more violent forms" (*Storia d'Italia*, 274). Futurism, like any form of decadent art, is the result of a "moral and intellectual dissolution" against which the intellectual is helpless: "All one can do is step aside and let the epidemic take its course" (275).

Croce's resigned attitude to Futurism is indebted once again to *secentismo*, to seventeenth-century thought, and to Torquato Accetto, who, in a little book discovered by Croce, *Della dissimulazione honesta* (Of honest dissimulation), advised how to deal with difficult times. Croce describes Accetto's technique of dissimulation as a triumph of the intellect over the emotions, by which man wins by winning over himself: "He [Accetto] demonstrates the role played by 'dissimulation' with which man controls the pointless and damaging outbursts of his emotions, and wins by virtue of his intelligence, and wins over himself, which is the greatest victory. And though he feels pain in keeping quiet about what he would like to say or in refraining from doing what is suggested by his feelings, with sobriety in words and deeds he overcomes the senses and achieves peace of mind" (*SEB*, 162). In his *Taccuini di lavoro* (Work diary), in the entry for 15 December 1926, referring once again to Accetto's treatise and in direct response to the political climate of Fascism at the time, Croce wrote: "Thus, one must live as if the world went or was going in conformity to our ideals. One must be reminded of that little seventeenth-century treatise that I discovered, *Della dissimulazione onesta*, of the self-deceit that one has the right and the duty to put into practice in order to bear life. So that we can provide some stability to our inner life." When those ideals concern art, poetry, and history, the result is negative history, the history of non-history, the history of a pseudo-poetics, of allegory; in other words, a history of error and deceit, a history of simulation of truth, of morality, and of ideals; in short, a history of the Baroque age in Italy.

Croce's history of the Baroque sums up very well the contradictions at the heart of his own philosophy and its close connection to aesthetics and to allegory. The critique of the Baroque as an age without poetry, in which poetry is silent, is an extension to history of his critique of allegory as pseudo-aesthetic and error. In this history of the Baroque, allegory is confined to a period in the hope that Croce may never see the likes of it again, although we know from *A Croce Reader*, as he did, that allegory is inseparable from art and that it is the nature and the essence of what is artistic in the Baroque or in any age.

"Barocco"
(*La storia dell'età barocca in Italia*, pp. 21–42)

[21] By now everyone says "Baroque age," "Baroque painting," and so on, and under the same label are placed together many things of the broadest quality: real painters as well as flashy and pseudo-painters, and likewise poets and non-poets, and so on. As a result people also say "a nice Baroque" or similar approbatory and admiring formulas. That is, one tends to give to the concept of baroque a positive meaning, or one alternates a positive meaning with a negative one. It would be futile to complain against this use of language; it is better to clarify the concept by going back to its origins.

The origins show that the term "baroque" and its concept originated with a disapproving intention to earmark not an epoch of the story of the Spirit and an art form, but a type of artistic perversion and ugliness. In my view, it is important that the term maintains or reassumes this function and meaning in the rigorous and scientific use of the term, expanding it and providing it with a better logical determination.

As for its origins, there is no doubt that the term is connected to one of those words artificially composed and memorialized with which medieval logic designated the figures of syllogisms. Among these terms (*Barbara, Celarent,* etc.) two of them stuck more than the others, at least in Italy, and became proverbial and were preferred to the others: the first, that is, *Barbara,* because it was the first one; and then, who knows why, *Baroco,* which designated the fourth manner of the second figure. I said I did not know because it was not stranger than the others, nor did it point to a more contorted form of syllogism. Perhaps, the alliteration with *Barbara* helped [...]

[25] Whatever one may think of the etymology of the word, it is certain that the concept of *barocco* was formed in art criticism to define a form of artistic bad taste that characterized in large part the architecture of the seventeenth century, but also its sculpture and painting. And it goes hand in hand with the way in which the dominant poetry and prose of the age was condemned as "bad taste" or "literary plague" or "delirium," and that in the twentieth century took the name of "seventeenth-century style" [secentismo], which it still retains today. And they go hand in hand so well that they are identical, and since we have been speaking of literary "Baroque" or "Baroquism" for a while now and calling Marini, Achillini, Battisti, and Artali "Baroque" poets, we should encourage this usage not only to consolidate the identity of this artistic flaw [vizio] in poetry and in the other arts, but also to avoid the inconvenience of paradoxical word combinations whereby we speak of "*secentismo*" in the fifteenth century, in the Latin decadent poets, and maybe even in the "Fathers of the Church."

Therefore, the "Baroque" is a kind of artistic ugly, and as such it has nothing artistic; on the contrary, it is something different from art from which it has falsified [mentito] the appearance and the name, and in whose place it has introduced or substituted itself. This something does not obey the laws of artistic coherence but rebels against them or deceives them, answering, as is obvious, to another law that can only be that of pleasure, comfort, and whim, and therefore is utilitarian or hedonistic. Thus the Baroque, as any type of artistic ugly, has its foundation in a practical need, whatever it may be, and however it may be formed, but in the cases with which we are concerned here it is simply formed by the demand and for the enjoyment of a thing that delights – against everything else and primarily against art itself.

[26] To differentiate the "Baroque" from other types of ugly or non-poetic forms one has to look for the type of hedonistic satisfaction to which it corresponds, being careful, however, that the search for this subject consists only of an empirical classification because of the infinite variety, the infinite tonalities or shades of pleasure. It is also clear that the various classes or types of pleasure that are listed under the non-poetic do not exclude each other; in fact, they combine with one another, where one calls for the other, as Manzoni remarked of his fictitious anonymous author of the seventeenth century whose prose was "both coarse and affected."

Indeed, it is not difficult to point out the characteristics of the Baroque – for instance the one that differentiates it, for instance, from the "academic" or from the "sentimental" or from the "mawkish" baroque, and which consists in substituting poetic truth and the enchantment that arises from it with the unexpected and the astonishing, which excites, intrigues, astonishes, and delights by means of the particular jolt that it provides. It is not difficult because, as is well known, this characteristic was expounded upon, programmatically, by the artists of that school and by their leader, Giambattista Marino, who declared that the aim of the poet was to create "wonder" and who warned those who could not create it to give up being poets and to take up work as stable hands. We could quote many examples here, but it would be superfluous. There were those who even then, in comparing the pure and ideal commotion required by poetry with that alien commotion, accused the modern poets of "seriously erring" in "matters of pathos" where, "by using elaborate concepts and witticisms of free and non-passionate spirits, it was not any wonder that they did not bond and did not make others passionate," as it was the case with Tasso who "got caught once" and with Marino who "very indecently fell into it" [...]

[28] The historians of art, of Baroque sculpture, painting, and architecture, are also aware of similar substitutions of harmonious palpitations and of contemplative artistic ecstasy for practical astonishment [...] Burckhardt speaks of the "pseudo-dramatic life" introduced both in sculpture and in painting so that where the feeling is not as deep and is less intimate, the more the drapery wreaks havoc, translating the pseudo-drama into the absurdity of its folds [...] Alois Riegl describes the puzzlement that the works provoke in those who regard them from

the aspect of art. "A figure is praying and is distorted in this act with spasmodic movements. Why these movements? They seem unmotivated, and we don't understand them. The skirt is inflated, violently moved as by a hurricane, and we ask, why? Nearby there is a tree whose leaves are completely at rest. Why does the hurricane move the skirt but not the leaves?" The reason is that the real coherence of the poetic and of artistic images has been replaced by a coherent incoherence with the sole aim of surprising people with the unexpected and the astonishing, however achieved [...]

[29] It is not necessary [...] to state the obvious and to demonstrate that the "Baroque" is this game and this rush to astonish. By its own nature, and different from other types of ugliness that sometimes stir, excite, and upset us, it is cold, despite its agitation and its superficial warmth, and leaves us with a sense of emptiness, despite the crowd of images and the combination of images that it puts into play. This also explains how sometimes it appears to pass from the most subtle intellectualism to the most crass realistic and naturalistic representations. It is impossible for the Baroque to represent a poetic image, which is spirit and body, feeling and figure, ideality and sensibility. All is left for the Baroque to do, which does not want to make poetry but to arouse astonishment, is either to broaden empty concepts in antitheses and other relations, as if to provide proof of spirituality and ideality, or to observe and reproduce the signs of things in their materiality and exteriority, as if to show its extraordinary plastic power and its realistic courage.

But this type of realism is intellectualistic, just as this spiritualism is materialistic. Before certain baroque sculptures, paintings, and poems everybody feels that these representations of the foul, the horrible, and the bloody, or even simply of ordinary and common life, have as their sole purpose the creation of admiration for having dared to reproduce what others would have never dared to do as a subject of art. Representation is description and skilled description. One is reminded of the example often quoted of Father Orchi's comparison of the act of confession with the work of a washerwoman. He takes his time to describe in every detail the work of the washerwoman who "having rolled up her sleeves, tucked in her sides, takes the dirty clothes and kneels by the river," and so on for many lines until "in four crumples, three shakes, two rinses, and a squeeze, the clothing comes out cleaner and more candid than before." In the Baroque the comic and the laughter are also characterized with some strain to represent an ultra-comic comic and laughter that is more laughter than usual, but, for this, it is no less frigid than the heroic or the passionate. A spontaneous and genuine laughter goes hand in hand with a seriousness of feeling and with the freedom of the mind that seeks peace.

When we examine a single baroque poem or a painting, we can show its poetic and artistic incoherence in its various parts or forms, and its coherence to pratico-hedonistic ends, as we have said. But we must be careful not to fall into the error of believing that certain types of [forms, when abstracted from their single works, belong to the Baroque, so that wherever we find them we assert the existence of the Baroque. [Croce mentions the examples of Caterina da Siena, Jakob Böhme, Angelus Silesius, Du Bartas, Gongora, and Romanticism.] [...]

[33] Understood within the general outline that we have described, the Baroque can be found in any place and any time, here and there, and more or less noticeable. It is an aesthetic sin [peccato estetico], but also a human sin, universal and perpetual, as all human sins, if anything because of the danger it presents. Similarly, as with Romanticism, one could construct a generic human or psychological concept, and on its basis discover Romanticism in any age and in every people, here and there [...] A similar comparison and a heated polemic have become fashionable in today's literature, both foreign and Italian, and particularly in D'Annunzio's work. I am not implying that these approaches are not legitimate or are pointless; on the contrary, I admit that they are of some use, judging by the fact that they are made spontaneously. Yet, even more useful, it seems to me, and not just for Romanticism but also for the Baroque, is to make use of the relative concept in its historical sense, and not simply psychologically, by referring it to what was directly instrumental in constructing it and in forging the relative term. Thus, one ought to understand the Baroque as that artistic perversion, dominated by the need for astonishment, which one observes in Europe roughly in the last years of the sixteenth and seventeenth centuries [...]

[35] It is important to employ the concepts of Baroque and Romanticism as historical concepts in order to avoid falling, precisely, into the indefinite, the meaningless, and finally falsehoods, misreading the physiognomy and the individual and proper character of the work under scrutiny. Even granted that in seventeenth-century French, Italian, or Spanish literature there may be some romantic moments (in the general sense that we indicated), these same works were intimately very different from the romantic works of the nineteenth century, because those were born in the seventeenth century and these in the

nineteenth century, after two centuries of mankind's life and spiritual struggle. Similarly, as I have already observed, all the baroque elements that we can observe in D'Annunzio, and all the similarities in Marino, do not erase the fact that a D'Annunzio could only have arisen after Romanticism, Verismo, Parnassianism, Nietzscheanism, and other spiritual events that certainly did not precede Marino, because they came to maturity in the nineteenth century.

At this point we must displease, once again, those who are always asking for the "cause" of events and who are not happy until they have been given a causal explanation, and therefore they are destined never to be contented. Our regret lies in the answer that, after all, the Baroque does not have a cause. Understood in a psychological or generic sense, the Baroque does not have a cause, because human error does not have a cause, unless we want to point to the *virtus dormitiva*, namely, the very same sinful nature of man. And there is not even a cause of the Baroque understood as a historical concept; the cause is the fact itself – in so far as it is a fact [...]

[37] If those who demand a cause have not been satisfied so far, I cannot satisfy them now, when asked why, between the sixteenth century and the end of the seventeenth century, did Europe sin so extensively in matters of good taste and produce so much Baroque. I would have to answer, simply, in homage to the freedom of the human spirit, that Europe worked that way because it wanted to work that way; it did what it wanted to do because it liked it that way [...]

[39] If the Baroque has neither an artistic nor a poetic character, but a practical one, both in a single work, and even more so in a school or in a style, which is already a practical act in itself, the historian of poetry and of art can only think of it negatively and not positively, that is, as a negation or a limitation of what is more properly art and poetry. One can use terms like "Baroque age" or "Baroque art," but one should never lose the conscience that, strictly speaking, what is truly art is never baroque, and what is baroque is not truly art [...] Throughout the Baroque age the historian of poetry and of art, therefore, will look for genuine art and poetry, but not for Baroque, and he will be able to recognize them even if sometimes they are found marked on the surface or by some traits of the ruling fashion, or if, in any case, they presuppose it and underline it [...]

[41] If, as did earlier generations, we still feel today an impatience and a dislike of these exaggerated forms, of the clever combinations that should create wonder for their over-abundant and complicated

metaphors and antitheses and for their witticisms and such, and if we are ready to discern, and to accuse, or to laugh at these things as "*secentismo*," "Baroque style," "*concettismo*," and so on, to whom do we owe this clarity of judgment and determination of principles but to that age that took upon itself all the sins that could be committed, and expiated them all? Even the Baroque age as Baroque, then, has not lived in vain.

Bibliography

Primary Sources

Listed here are the original texts that have been translated in
A Croce Reader. As indicated in the introduction, the published
English translations have not been used.

Croce, Benedetto. *Ariosto, Shakespeare e Corneille*. Bari: Laterza & Figli, 1917,
1961. Translated by Douglas Ainslie as *Ariosto, Shakespeare and Corneille*
[New York: Russell & Russell, 1966].
– *Breviario di estetica. Quattro lezioni*. Bari: Laterza, 1913. Translated by Hiroko
Fudemoto, with an introduction by Remo Bodei, as *Breviary of Aesthetics:
Four Lectures* [Toronto: University of Toronto Press, 2007].
– *Estetica come scienza dell'espressione e linguistica generale*. Bari: Laterza & Figli, 1902,
1965. Translated by Colin Lyas as *The Aesthetic as the Science of Expression and of
the Linguistic in General* [Cambridge: Cambridge University Press, 1902, 1922].
– *Filosofia, poesia, storia: Pagine tratte da tutte le opere, a cura dell'autore*. Milan,
Naples: Riccardo Ricciardi, 1951; reissued by Adelphi Edizioni, Milan, 1996.
Translated, with an introduction, by Cecil Sprigge as *Philosophy, Poetry, History:
An anthology of essays* [London, New York: Oxford University Press, 1966].
– *La filosofia di G.B. Vico*. Bari: Laterza & Figli, 1911, 1962. Translated by R.G.
Collingwood as *The Philosophy of Giambattista Vico* [New York: Russell &
Russell, 1964].
– "L'Intuizione pura e il carattere lirico dell'arte." In *Problemi di Estetica e
contributi alla storia dell'Estetica Italiana*, 1–30. Bari: Laterza & Figli, 1954.
– *Logica come scienza del concetto puro*. Naples: Bibliopolis, 1908, 1996.
Translated by Douglas Ainslie as *Logic as the Science of the Pure Concept*
[London: Macmillan, 1917].

– "Necessità di tornare al De Sanctis." In *Pagine sparse*, vol. 3, 272–3. Bari: Laterza & Figli, 1960.
– "Pensieri sull'arte dell'avvenire." In *L'Italia dal 1914 al 1918: Pagine sulla Guerra*, 270–5. Bari: Laterza & Figli, 1950.
– "Pirandello." In *La letteratura della nuova Italia*, vol. 6, 354–73. Bari: Laterza & Figli, 1957.
– *La poesia: Introduzione alla critica della poesia e della letteratura*. Milan: Adelphi, 1936, 1994. Translated by Giovanni Gullace as *Benedetto Croce's Poetry and Literature: An Introduction to Its Criticism and History* [Carbondale: Southern Illinois University Press, 1981].
– *La poesia di Dante*. Bari: Laterza & Figli, 1920, 1966. Translated by Douglas Ainslie as *The Poetry of Dante* [New York: Paul P. Appel, 1971].
– "Rigoglio di cultura e irrequietezza spirituale (1901–1914)." In *Storia d'Italia dal 1871 al 1915*, ed. Giuseppe Galasso, 309–31. Milan: Adelphi, 1991.
– *Saggio sullo Hegel*. Bari: Laterza & Figli, 1906, 1967. Translated by Douglas Ainslie as *What Is Living and What Is Dead of the Philosophy of Hegel* [New York: Russell & Russell, 1969].
– *La storia come pensiero e come azione*. Naples: Bibliopolis, 1938, 2003. Translated by S. Sprigge as *History as the Story of Liberty* [New York: Noonday Press, 1955].
– *Storia dell'età barocca in Italia: Pensiero – Poesia – e letteratura; Vita morale*. Bari: Laterza & Figli, 1957.
– "Sulla natura dell'allegoria." In *Nuovi saggi di Estetica*, 331–8. Bari: Laterza & Figli, 1922, 1969.
– *Teoria e storia della storiografia*. Milan: Adelphi, 1916, 1989. Translated by Douglas Ainslie as *History: Its Theory and Practice* [New York: Russell & Russell, 1921 1960]. Published in England in 1921 with the title *Theory and History of Historiography*.

Secondary Sources

Prete, Antonio. *La distanza da Croce*. Milan: Celuc, 1970.
Sasso, Gennaro. *Per invigilare me stesso: I Taccuini di lavoro di Benedetto Croce*. Bologna: Il Mulino, 1989.
Serra Renato. "Le Lettere." In *Scritti letterari, morali e politici: Saggi e articoli dal 1900 al 1915*, ed. Mario Isnenghi, 363–482. Turin: Giulio Einaudi,1974.

Selected Critical Studies

Caponigri, A. Robert. *History and Liberty: The Historical Writings of Benedetto Croce*. London: Routledge and Kegan Paul, 1955.

Gullace, Giovanni. Translator's Introduction to *Benedetto Croce's Poetry and Literature: An Introduction to His Criticism and History*. Carbondale: Southern Illinois University Press, 1981.

Moss, M.E. *Benedetto Croce Reconsidered: Truth and Error in Theories of Art, Literature, and History*. Hanover, NH: University Press of New England, 1987.

– *Essays on Literature and Literary Criticism*. Annotated and translated from the Italian with an introduction. Albany: State University of New York Press, 1990.

Orsini, Gian N.G. *Benedetto Croce: Philosopher of Art and Literary Critic*. Carbondale: Southern Illinois University Press, 1961.

Palmer, L.M., and H.S. Harris, eds. *Thought, Action and Intuition: A Symposium on the Philosophy of Benedetto Croce*. Hildesheim and New York: Georg Olms Verlag, 1975.

Parente, Alfredo. *Croce per lumi sparsi*. Florence: La nuova Italia, 1975.

Paolozzi, Ernesto. *Aesthetics as a Form of Knowledge*. Translated by Emanuele Paparella. Ovi Symposium on "Arte, filosofia, umanesimo." *Ovi Magazine*, 2013.

– *Logic of the Real and the Duty of Liberty*. Translated by M. Verdicchio. An e-book (2013).

Pirandello, Luigi. "L'umorismo." In *Saggi, poesie, scritti*. Edited by Manlio Lo Vecchio Musti. Milan: Mondadori, 1973.

Rizi, Fabio F. *Benedetto Croce and Italian Fascism*. Toronto: University of Toronto Press, 2003.

Roberts, D. David. *Benedetto Croce and the Uses of Historicism*. Berkeley: University of California Press, 1987.

– *Historicism and Fascism in Modern Italy*. Toronto: University of Toronto Press, 2007.

– *Nothing but History: Reconstruction and Extremity after Metaphysics*. Berkeley: University of California Press, 1995.

Sprigge, C. *Benedetto Croce: Man and Thinker*. New Haven, CT: Yale University Press, 1952.

Verdicchio, Massimo. *Naming Things: Aesthetics, Philosophy, and History in Benedetto Croce*. Naples: La città del Sole, 2000.

Wellek, René. "The concept of Baroque in Literary Scholarship." *Journal of Aesthetics and Literary Criticism* 5, December 1946, no. 2, 77–109.

White, Hayden V. *Metahistory: The Historical Imagination in Nineteenth-Century Europe*. Baltimore, MD: Johns Hopkins University Press, 1973.

For a more comprehensive bibliography on Croce consult
the above works by Moss, Roberts, and White.